Faith doesn't come by itself.
You must work for it.

Isaac Bashevis Singer

Through the deep caves of thought I hear
a voice that sings: —
Build thee more stately mansions, O my
soul,
As the swift seasons roll!

Oliver Wendell Holmes
from the poem "Chambered Nautilus," 1857.

To

the memory of

G. Edward MacFarlane

a good friend and colleague

MORE STATELY MANSIONS
Churches of Nova Scotia 1830-1910

by ELIZABETH PACEY with George Rogers and Allan Duffus

LANCELOT PRESS
Hantsport, Nova Scotia

ACKNOWLEDGMENT

This book has been published with the assistance of the Nova Scotia Department of Culture, Recreation and Fitness.

ISBN 0-88999-210-X

Published November, 1983
Second printing September 1984

LANCELOT PRESS LIMITED, Hantsport, N.S.

ACKNOWLEDGEMENTS

The authors would like to acknowledge the support and encouragement of many organizations and individuals. We are grateful for the financial assistance received from the Nova Scotia Department of Culture, Recreation and Fitness which helped with research expenses. We would like to thank the staff of the Public Archives of Nova Scotia who were always friendly and co-operative.

Special thanks go to Dr. Philip Pacey for reading the manuscript and for willingly driving around Nova Scotia so that the churches might be surveyed. We extend thanks to Mrs. Kay MacIntosh and Mr. Tim Randall for lending relevant books from their personal libraries. Mr. Tim Randall also provided necessary photographs as did Mrs. Elizabeth Ross and Mr. Robert Gourley. We offer thanks, too, to Patricia Hatt and Carol Denton for expertly typing the manuscript.

Many people throughout the province provided valuable information and assistance on the individual churches. We sincerely thank the following persons for this help: Mrs. E. B. Fairbanks and Mr. Hugh A. MacDonald (St. Mary's, Lismore); Rev. E. Richard (St. James', Sherbrooke); Mrs. E. A. Marshall (Clarence United Baptist); Rev. Stanley MacDonald and Mrs. Margaret MacIsaac (St. Margaret's, Broad Cove); Mrs. Everett Fraser (St. Andrew's, Gairloch); Mrs. Garfield Johnston (St. John's, MacLennan's Mountain); Father Ray Huntley and Father Charles Brewer (St. Ninian's Cathedral, Antigonish); Rev. E. C. Sturge (Fort Massey, Halifax); Mr. and Mrs. John A. Beaton and Hugh MacDonald (St. Joseph's, Glencoe Mills); Mr. Walter Tucker and Mrs. Catherine Thompson (Westminster, New Glasgow); Dr. C. M. Bethune, Mr. Tim Randall, Rev. F. W. Peacock and Mr. Niels Jannasch (Gibbons' Churches); Marion Giddens (St. James', Great Village); Rev. William E. Dyke and Dean E. B. N. Cochrane (St. James', Mahone Bay); Mr. St. Clair Bentley (Peniel United, Five Islands); Rev. Gerald Saulnier (St. Ambrose Cathedral, Yarmouth); Mrs. Wentworth MacLean (St. John's, Strathlorne); and Rev. John E. Boyd (First Baptist, Amherst). Both Mr. James St. Clair and Mrs. Norma McKay provided very helpful information on Cape Breton churches in general. Once again, we would like to acknowledge Rev. Dr. M. Allen Gibson's extensive series of newspaper articles, *Churches by the Sea*, which has greatly helped our project.

CONTENTS

Introduction 13

Regional Design 17

Churches

St. Anne's, Bear River 33
St. Mary's, Lismore 39
St. Paul's, Rawdon 45
St. James', Sherbrooke 51
Clarence United Baptist 57
St. Margaret's, Broad Cove 63
St. Andrew's, Gairloch 69
St. Matthew's, Halifax 75
St. John's, MacLennan's Mountain 81
St. Ninian's Cathedral, Antigonish 87
Fort Massey, Halifax 95
St. Joseph's, Glencoe Mills 103
Westminster, New Glasgow 107
Gibbons' Churches: Baddeck, Jordon Falls,
Diligent River, Moose River 113
St. James', Great Village 121
St. James', Mahone Bay 127
Peniel United, Five Islands 133
St. Ambrose Cathedral, Yarmouth 139
Eglise St. Pierre, Cheticamp 145
St. John's, Strathlorne 151
First Baptist, Amherst 155
Eglise Ste-Marie, Church Point 161

Appendix and Glossary 169

Bibliography and Credits 181

INTRODUCTION

More Stately Mansions is a companion volume to *Thy Dwellings Fair*, which outlined the historical and architectural significance of Nova Scotia's earliest churches, built in the Georgian period from 1750 to 1830. This second volume deals with the churches of the next 80-year building period, including the Victorian and Edwardian eras, and completes this survey of historic churches in the province.

The study of architectural styles for this period was far more complicated than for the Georgian era. This was due to the large number of churches built throughout the province during the period.

In order to trace the evolution of architectural designs and to determine if regional differences existed within the province, a county by county survey of 577 historic churches was conducted. While not every church of the period was included, a large enough number in each county was studied to indicate stylistic similarities and variations. The results of the survey are contained in the Appendix, wherein each church visited is listed and categorized according to its style. The chapter on Regional Design attempts to analyze the findings, by noting major design trends and regional characteristics.

For *Thy Dwellings Fair*, the selection of churches to be documented was straightforward, as relatively few churches exist from the 1750-1830 period in Nova Scotia; the 22 churches chosen represented about 80 per cent of the total. In contrast, the 22 churches selected for detailed discussion in this volume represent only a small percentage of the churches surveyed.

The churches were chosen on the basis of selection criteria. There is at least one church for every decade in order to provide a range of ages. A variety of styles was also included, as well as an indication of the progression of styles from the beginning of the era to the end. Each of the major regions of the province, such as Cape Breton, the South Shore and the French Shore, has at least one representative. The various denominations were represented if possible, with emphasis on those denominations that were dominant in the period. For example, the 1871 census showed that there were 103,539 Presbyterians, 102,001 Roman Catholics, 73,430 Baptists, 55,430 Anglicans, and 36,683 Methodists in Nova Scotia. Therefore, the majority of churches selected for this volume were of Presbyterian and Roman Catholic origin. The historical importance of the churches was also taken into account. Churches were chosen to represent the work of various architects of the period. Finally, churches that had been unsympathetically changed were not chosen. For example, churches with modern siding were not considered, as such siding mars the appearance of an historic church.

The 22 churches which have been documented are an indication of the variety of historic church architecture in Nova Scotia. There are many churches of equal significance which have not been included in this book because of space constraints. Nevertheless, it is hoped that *More Stately Mansions* will promote an awareness of churches and their styles, which constitute a rich historical resource in Nova Scotia.

REGIONAL DESIGN

Prior to 1830, a particular style of church architecture had developed. The early style, which was used throughout Nova Scotia, was, in essence, a blending of the New England meeting house design with elements of British classical architecture. Typically, a Georgian church would be a rectangular wooden structure, symmetrical in form, with a pitched roof and central steeple. Classical ornamentation such as round-headed windows, corner pilasters and pediments would be incorporated into the design. This style evolved from the earliest Nova Scotia churches like St. Paul's in Halifax, built in 1750, or St. Mary's at Auburn, built in 1791.

Between 1830 and 1910, the most prolific church building period in the province's history, three major trends occurred. Firstly, Gothic architecture became more popular in Nova Scotia because of a revival of interest in medieval Gothic architecture in Britain. In this province, the Gothic style manifested itself in two ways. Gothic embellishments such as pointed windows, ornamental buttresses and finials became more common. Prior to 1830, the only Gothic feature was the use of pointed windows on a few otherwise classical churches. But from the mid-19th century, Gothic detailing became more prevalent and more lavish. As well, the trend to the Gothic style in Nova Scotia meant the increased use of unsymmetrical configurations. Steeples and main entrances were placed in off-centre positions, or towers of differing heights might have been used. However, while the Gothic style in Nova Scotia may have changed the layout and decoration of churches, it was not a fundamental structural change as it had been in medieval times; then, in the late 12th century, the discovery of the pointed arch and supporting buttresses had made a "skeletal" system of construction possible and allowed for much higher buildings and larger windows.

Secondly, denominational preferences for certain styles became more pronounced. The Roman Catholics preferred the traditional Nova Scotia style as well as Romanesque and Baroque styles. The Anglicans, who were the originators of the traditional classical style, switched, almost exclusively, to unsymmetrical styles with Gothic detailing. This switch took place after 1850. The Lutherans were also partial to the unsymmetrical styles, while the Baptists, Presbyterians, Methodists and Congregationalists preferred the plain meeting house and traditional, classical styles.

The third major trend was the emergence of regional styles within Nova Scotia that sometimes overruled denominational preferences. One reason for the evolution of regional styles may have been that the same builder or builders constructed churches of various denominations in a given area. This is likely the case in Lunenburg County. However, in other instances, a popular style used by various builders in an area may simply be attributed to a regional preference. This is true in Pictou County where a particular meeting house style prevailed for at least three decades with different builders involved.

Regional designs are often variations of the traditional Nova Scotia style or of a style preferred by a particular denomination. Regional designs may be expressed in terms of the type of embellishments on the church structure, or may depend on the actual form or plan of the building, whether symmetrical or unsymmetrical. Another factor which influenced regional styles is the date of construction. For example, the mid-19th century styles of Hants County are more traditional than the unsymmetrical styles found in Lunenburg County, where the construction of churches flourished around the turn of the century.

Further general observations may also be made about this building period. It was, for instance, the era when the architectural profession became established and began to design churches, particularly in the urban centres. In the previous building period, churches had been designed by carpenters and master builders. While wood still remained the most-used medium for church construction, more stone and brick structures took shape, especially in the towns and cities. For example, a number of brick churches were built in Halifax.

Construction methods became more sophisticated. For example, early foundations were often made of rubble-stone without the benefit of mortar, or granite blocks hauled to the site; later foundations were made of brick or neatly cut stone held together with mortar. Towards the end of the period, great feats of building took place. The small scale of the early churches had gradually led to larger churches and finally to monumental edifices.

The following paragraphs attempt to define the various regional styles of church architecture in Nova Scotia from 1830 to 1910.

Cape Breton

Cape Breton Island encompasses the four counties of Richmond, Cape Breton, Victoria and Inverness. The rural areas of Richmond and Cape Breton counties have a majority of Roman Catholic congregations while Victoria County is mainly Protestant with emphasis on the Presbyterian and United denominations. Rural Inverness County is almost equally divided between Roman Catholic and Protestant (generally United Church) congregations. In the urban areas, all denominations are represented, though they do not all have churches from the period.

In rural Cape Breton Island, the dominant architectural design is similar to the traditional Nova Scotia style of the Georgian period, with the exception that the windows generally have Gothic arches. This version of the traditional style is so prevalent that it crosses county as well as denominational lines.

The earliest and most classical examples of the traditional style in rural Cape Breton are found in St. Mary's Roman Catholic Church built at East Bay, Cape

Breton County, in 1837, and St. Margaret of Scotland Roman Catholic Church, built in 1841 at River Denys Mountain. In both cases, the steeples are reminiscent of the Georgian, Wren style with square towers and octagonal lanterns topped with rounded roofs and slim spires. The River Denys Mountain church also has round-headed classical windows with primitive pediments.

As the style evolved the windows, doors and belfry openings more often had Gothic arches than rounded ones, but the detailing at the corners, gables and doorways remained classical. Some fine examples of the style are St. Mary's of the Angels, Glendale (pictured), and St. Margaret's Roman Catholic, Broad Cove, both in Inverness County, as well as Ephraim Scott Memorial Presbyterian at South Gut, St. Ann's and St. Andrew's Presbyterian at North River Bridge in Victoria County. In Richmond County, the Church of the Immaculate Conception, at Simon River, is also a good example, as is St. Columba Presbyterian at Marion Bridge in Cape Breton County.

In the urban areas, the unsymmetrical plans with side steeples and Gothic detailing are more common. This is partly because the churches are of a later date. For example, in North Sydney, Sydney Mines, and Glace Bay, the majority of the churches of the period were built after the turn of the century. A further reason for the stylistic change in the urban areas is the greater degree of sophistication. The Sacred Heart Roman Catholic Church built in 1883 in Sydney (pictured) illustrates this fact. While the design of the higher belfry and spire have elements of the traditional rural style, the double asymmetrical steeples and corner buttresses add a sophisticated flourish.

Pictou and Antigonish Counties

The churches of rural Pictou County are an interesting phenomenon. There are eleven or more country churches that are built in a similar style. The popular style, of which St. John's at MacLennan's Mountain is a good example, is a simple meeting house with no steeple and long rectangular windows. Decorative features usually include classical corner pilasters, a small gable window and a moulded panel above the front door. Interestingly enough, this meeting house style was used by different builders for at least a thirty-year period during the 1850's, 1860's and 1870's. For example, Donald Grant was the builder of the MacLennan's Mountain meeting house in 1860, while Hugh and Alexander Chisholm were the builders of Blair Presbyterian at Garden of Eden in 1873. Variations on this style occur in West River Presbyterian at Durham, First Presbyterian at Hopewell and St. George's Presbyterian at River John where a long square central tower with a long rectangular window has been added to the front facade.

In contrast to the plain, classical meeting houses like Blair Presbyterian, the highly ornamented Gothic Westminster Church was built in New Glasgow about the same time.

The second most popular style, found both in the towns and country areas, is a variation of the traditional Nova Scotia style. Like St. Andrew's at Gairloch, both the main structure and the saddle-back tower feature Gothic openings. Finials are often used at the corners and atop the tower; octagonal belfries and spires may also top off the square tower. First Presbyterian in Pictou, St. Andrew's (Kirk) Church in New Glasgow and Christ Church Anglican in Stellarton, illustrate these features.

Antigonish County has a relatively small land area and population. As well, the county is largely Roman Catholic and hence, has fewer, but larger, churches. The predominant rural style is, like that of Cape Breton, the traditional symmetrical configuration, a central steeple with octagonal belfry and spire, Gothic window arches and some classical detailing.

The Eastern Shore

In Halifax County along the Eastern Shore, the majority of the churches surveyed have an unsymmetrical configuration with a tower at the side of the main structure. This is quite unusual as the predominant configuration in the other counties is more often symmetrical. This unsymmetrical form is further defined by a very distinctive tiered steeple style which appears on a number of churches. Typically, the first tier is the square tower which contains the main entrance and is finished by a long four-sided bellcast roof, punctuated by a peaked dormer hood on each side. The second tier consists of an open or partially open belfry topped by a short flared roof and an octagonal spire above. The

architectural details, such as door, window, and belfry openings, are generally Gothic on churches of this style. A good example of the style is St. John's Anglican at Oyster Pond. In fact, most of the churches with the tiered steeple are Anglican, but the style does cross denominational lines as it is also found at St. Denis Roman Catholic Church at East Ship Harbour (pictured).

Continuing along the Eastern Shore and into Guysborough County, the predominant architectural configuration again becomes symmetrical. Certainly the United and Roman Catholic churches are built in symmetrical forms with only a few exceptions. The Baptists have used the symmetrical plan more often than the unsymmetrical and even the Anglicans have more symmetrical churches in Guysborough County.

In spite of the widespread use of the symmetrical configuration, the details, such as window, door or belfry openings are generally Gothic. In the mid-19th century, small, many-paned muntined Gothic arch windows without label mouldings were popular (pictured). The United Church in Boylston, built in 1847, and St. James' Anglican in Sherbrooke, which was built in 1850, both have this simple, yet very attractive, window type.

Another Gothic feature, which appeared later in the 19th century, is the hooded dormer belfry opening used on an octagonal, pointed spire just above the wide flare of the roof. Such belfry openings are found on Anglican, Baptist and Roman Catholic churches. St. James' Anglican at Halfway Cove, and St. Bartholomew's at Cole Harbour, illustrate this type of belfry opening.

Hants, Cumberland and Colchester

These three counties in central Nova Scotia have been grouped together because of certain architectural similarities in the mid-19th century churches of the rural areas. The meeting house style with no steeple, for instance, was popular with the Baptist and United Church denominations in the three counties. The Lower Selma Meeting House Museum (pictured) on the Noel Shore in Hants County is a particularly attractive illustration. The front elevation shows a pedimented gable with rondel window, and round-headed window and door arches with label mouldings. In Cumberland County, the Baptist meeting house at Amherst Point, built in 1853, has a pedimented gable with triangular window, decorative pilasters, and two entrance doors. The two separate entrance doors are also found on the Diligent River meeting house and the Lorneville United Church, built in 1863, in Cumberland County; in Hants County, the Bramber and Cambridge United Baptist meeting houses, as well as the Pembroke United Church (pictured) all have two front doors.

The Pembroke United Church also illustrates two other features that are common to Hants County. One feature is the saddle-back belfry, and the other is the triple-arch, Gothic window under the front gable. This type of decorative window with moulding, in the English Perpendicular Gothic style, is also found on the two Falmouth churches. The

saddle-back belfry, with or without a spire, is the most frequently used style in the rural areas. Notable examples are St. Paul's at Rawdon, Church of the Holy Spirit at Lakelands and the Kempt United Church.

In Colchester County, too, there are several meeting houses which are slightly plainer and of a larger scale than those of Hants and Cumberland counties. The Union Church at Bayhead is a good example. On the Parrsboro shore of Colchester County, the churches tend to be fairly individualistic and more decorative than those in the rest of the county. The Peniel Church at Five Islands and St. James' United in Great Village are the best examples.

In the various towns of the three counties, particularly Truro, Amherst, Springhill and Windsor, the churches are more elaborate than their rural counterparts. There are stone churches in all four towns, and in Amherst, there are two stone edifices, including the superb First Baptist Church.

The South Shore

The church architecture of the South Shore is extremely rich and varied. The churches themselves are numerous, particularly as the various Protestant denominations flourish in the area. Joining the Anglican, United, Presbyterian and Baptist congregations in Lunenburg County are the Lutherans who have many interesting historic churches.

In Lunenburg County, the major church building period was around the turn of the century. Approximately an equal number of churches were built in an unsymmetrical configuration with an off-centre tower as were built in a symmetrical configuration with a centred tower. One eye-catching feature which occurs frequently throughout the county, regardless of the general configuration or position of the steeple, is an open, cage-style belfry. The open cage belfry is very versatile; it is sometimes surmounted by a tall spire, sometimes topped by finials, or capped off by a short peaked roof.

There are many excellent examples of this belfry type. In Rose Bay, Trinity United, built in 1897 (pictured), displays two versions of the open cage belfry, although the taller belfry had a spire above until recent years. St.

James' Anglican at LaHave and St. Matthew's Evangelical Lutheran at Rose Bay (pictured) have very picturesque steeples with open cage belfries that still retain the tall spires. It is interesting that St. Matthew's and Trinity were built in 1897 by George W. Boehner while St. James was built a few years later, in 1905, by the Boehner Brothers. It is highly probable that the Boehners were very active in Lunenburg County and built a great many of the churches with open cage belfries.

A second style or variation of the belfry is also found in Lunenburg County. It has open classical or Gothic arches and a gabled or peaked top. St. Matthew's Presbyterian at West Dublin, St. Matthew's United at Broad Cove and St. John's United at Middle LaHave are examples.

Queen's County has far fewer churches than either Lunenburg or Shelburne counties. This is understandable as Queen's has, in fact, the smallest concentration of population of any county in the province. Nevertheless, the churches are historically interesting and include a range of architectural styles. The Old Meeting House at Port Medway dates from 1832 when it was built by Free Will Baptists. Its small scale and plain style, with straight-backed pews that face each other inside, depict the strict faith of the pioneer builders. All Saints' Anglican in Mill Village was built in 1861 in the country gothic style with a bell-cote, as was the Anglican Church of the Holy Redeemer in Port Medway.

Shelburne County has a larger number of historic churches with a high concentration of Baptist and United (formerly Methodist or Congregational) congregations. The churches are very decorative, displaying a great variety of embellishments, both classical and Gothic. The Chapel Hill Museum Church, built in 1856 at Shag Harbour, features a double classical pilaster at the corners of the structure. The Ragged Island Baptist Church at Osborne has a mansard-style belfry with hipped roof dormers that are common in Burgundy, France. This Burgundian style of belfry dormer is also found on the church at Roseway.

Temple United Baptist Church at Barrington displays peaked Gothic pediments along the edge of the roof. Small peaked dormers also appear on the Sable River United Baptist Church. Intricate flower motifs are found inside the dormer peaks and in the rondel windows of the front gable and tower. Another decorative feature of this church is the "fish-scale" or scalloped shingle patterns on the front gable and tower. This technique of cutting shingles in various shapes and designs, called "feathering," is very prevalent in Shelburne County. Shingle patterns include the "fish scale", "diamond" and "wavy" designs. The decorative shingle patterns are often used to accent a gable or steeple, and sometimes two or even three of the patterns are used together. Louis Head United Baptist, Jordan Falls United Baptist and South Side United Baptist have "fish-scale" shingle patterns, while Little Harbour United Church has a combination of three shingle designs which decorate the front gable and steeple. Holy Trinity Anglican at Jordan Falls (pictured) displays "diamond" shingle patterns.

Yarmouth and Digby Counties

The majority of the congregations in Yarmouth County are either Roman Catholic or Baptist. Both of these denominations prefer the classical or symmetrical configuration. Consequently, there are about twice as many symmetrical church plans as unsymmetrical in the county. The detailing is often classical too, though not always. Gothic embellishment is found on the large, Roman Catholic, Eglise Saint Pierre, built in 1888, at Middle West Pubnico.

However, Sainte Anne Roman Catholic Church, built in 1900, at Ste.-Anne-du-Ruisseau (pictured) had a great deal of classical detailing, including round-headed window arches and rondel tower windows, all with ornamental keystones. The central pedimented gable is flanked by twin towers. Double towers are popular in Yarmouth County and are found on Roman Catholic churches built from about the turn of the century and into the 1920's and 30's. Double towers were built in 1901 on the Buttes-Amirault Roman Catholic Church and St. Ambrose Cathedral in Yarmouth. Double towers are also found on Temple United Baptist Church built in 1870, and Zion United Baptist, built in 1895, both in the town of Yarmouth.

The Baptists generally used classical detailing. The Central Chebogue United Baptist Church (pictured), built in 1841, is a fine example. It is a simple meeting house, which is characteristic of early Baptist churches, but there is a great deal of classical ornamentation. The front gable is pedimented with prominent moulding and dentil trim (square, tooth-like decoration). The main structure also has corner pilasters. The embellishments are repeated on the front porch projection.

Digby County has a striking range of building styles, from small rural Protestant churches to the grand Roman Catholic churches of the French Shore.

Of the Protestant churches, by far the most numerous are Baptist, with a few Anglican, United (formerly Methodist), and Christian churches. The most characteristic style is the symmetrical configuration with a central tower and centre door flanked by a window on each side.

The windows usually have Gothic arches and are often the very pointed variety. Almost without exception the windows are accented by an "eyebrow" or label moulding detail above. However, while the windows are usually Gothic, the decorative detailing tends to be classical.

The oldest churches in the county contain the simpler and more traditional elements of the meeting house and classical styles. The Old Baptist Meeting House at Smith's Cove, built in 1838, has corner

pilasters and returns as well as entablatures over the doors. In Sandy Cove, the Nativity Anglican Church, built in 1844, is very clearly a meeting house with plain many-paned rectangular windows. Also at Sandy Cove, the United Baptist Church gives a sense of the classical meeting house tradition.

One feature which is quite unusual and particular to Digby County is the slanted-top corner pilaster. This detail is found on both churches at Centreville, the Lansdowne Baptist meeting house, and the Smith's Cove United Church. Built in 1885, Smith's Cove United features slanted-top pilasters at the corners of the main structure as well as on the steeple.

On the French Shore, the three churches of the 1830-1910 period were built on a grand scale, and are capable of seating more than 1000 persons apiece. At Saulnierville, Eglise Sacré-Coeur, built in 1880, maintains a symmetrical configuration with a central tower. St. Mary's, at Church Point, was begun in 1903 and is a veritable masterpiece of French Romanesque style. Just a few miles along the road, St. Bernard's is a monumental example of Gothic architecture.

Annapolis Valley

In the Annapolis Valley, there are several very early churches from the Georgian period between 1750 and 1830; there are also a fairly large number of churches from the Victorian period. Baptist, Anglican and United are the main denominations, and one finds a range of styles for each denomination. For example, there are simple Baptist meeting houses with no steeple and little embellishment found at Granville Beach, Mount Rose, Mount Hanley and Margaretsville in Annapolis County, and at West Hall's Harbour in Kings County. In contrast, one also finds later Gothic Baptist churches at Paradise, Annapolis Royal, Bridgetown and Middleton in Annapolis County and at Cambridge and Billtown in Kings County.

The Anglican churches from this period are generally unsymmetrical, with a side tower and Gothic windows, like Christ Church, Morden, in Kings County, or they may have a bell-cote, as do Holy Trinity at Middleton in Annapolis County and Christ Church at Berwick in Kings County. However, St. Andrew's Anglican at Lawrencetown, built in 1845, still maintains the classical plan of the earlier Anglican churches built in the Georgian period.

The United Churches in the Valley are usually unsymmetrical in form, particularly in the more populated centres. Bridgetown and Lawrencetown United Churches, in Annapolis County, or Trinity United in Canning, Kings County, are examples. Symmetrical styles, often with a mixture of Gothic and classical details, are still found in the less populated areas. Examples may be found at Clementsport, Margaretsville or Wilmot in Annapolis County, and at Morden, Harbourville and Scott's Bay in Kings County.

CHURCHES

St. Anne's, Bear River

Just outside Bear River, Digby County, on the wooded lands of the Indian Reservation, stands St. Anne's Roman Catholic Chapel. Its peaceful setting and antique air give little hint of the story of its construction, and the early 19th century attitudes towards the native people.

In a file of brittle, tattered documents, the story unfolds. On October 22, 1828, Judge Peleg Wiswall of Digby described in a letter the setting up of the first Indian reservation in the province. "The settlement forming between the forks of Bear River . . . is one of my own planning," he noted, adding, " . . . I have had the kind patronage of our late most excellent Governor (Sir James Kempt) as also that of your present Secretary Sir Rupert George." Judge Wiswall went on to explain that the settlement was "experimental, but should it succeed (it) will be copied as a pattern" and that "the Government has made suitable reserves of land in various parts of the Province."

Judge Wiswall may have been well-meaning. Certainly the land was good for hunting, trapping and fishing, and each family was given "a distinct allotment of about thirty acres." But his intolerance to the Indian lifestyle was unmistakable. He referred to their "harmful prejudices and superstitions" and their "careless habits" as well as "their living in temporary wigwams." He clearly stated that the main purpose of the settlement is "gradually to attach them to fixed abodes" and to "give them dispositions for tasting what we consider the sweets of life." He also threatened that the Indians "must have their natural propensities altered, or be very shortly utterly extinguished, for we have no room for wild men."

Two years later, on February 12, 1830, Judge Wiswall signed a further document outlining that the Indian families were "under guidance of Andrew Mewse, an intelligent Indian, and under the protection of the Government." He also noted that the Indians had "improved their several lots, considering their means, full as well as could reasonably be expected." He then proposed to erect a small chapel "as a means of further endearing the station to these simple suffering creatures, and gradually calling them off from their wild pursuits, to the comforts and security of more civilized life."

At this point, plans for the chapel had progressed quite far. For instance, a suitable piece of land had been set aside and consecrated. As well, Judge Wiswall had received an estimate of approximately £150 for "a building forty-five feet in length by twenty-five in breath, and thirteen in height with a plain pitch roof . . ." Judge Wiswall also noted certain interesting construction details as part of the estimate. Apparently he wanted "the whole outward surface, sides and ends as well as roof, to be well barked and shingled." Along with bark insulation and shingles he also stipulated that the window frames and corner boards were to be painted and "the rest white-washed."

A plaque inside the church states that Abbé Sigogne "blessed and laid the first stone" on August 19, 1831. Abbé Jean-Mandé Sigogne was a much-loved and respected Roman Catholic priest of the Acadian mission at St. Mary's Bay and Cape Sable. Born in Beaulieu, France, he was ordained in 1787, and served as a curate in the diocese of Tours. In 1790, his refusal to sign documents declaring the French Church separate from the Pope in Rome, led him to exile in England where he worked as a carpenter and learned to speak English fluently. In 1799, he emigrated to Nova Scotia to serve the Acadian mission of southwest Nova Scotia.

Abbé Sigogne also ministered to the native people in the area. At the age of 40, he taught himself the Micmac language in order to communicate better with his flock. A born singer, he instructed the Indians in religious music. When he heard them sing Mass for the first time, he joyfully wrote the Bishop, "I have never heard music so impressive even in the old cathedral at Tours."

The two men, Abbé Sigogne and Judge Wiswall, although they had quite different views about the native people, together became the commissioners of the Indian Chapel. As such, they administered the construction of the building.

A look at the accounts, bills received and paid by the Commissioners, presents an interesting picture of construction in the early 19th century. The lengthiest invoice of May, 1831, from the builder, William Farnham, lists his own expenses of drawing the plans at 16 shillings and 24 1/2 days of labour at 8 shillings and sixpence per day. As well, wages for seven workmen are listed along with costs of other items such as 150 pine beams from John Harris, 30 lb. of shingle nails from Stewart & Budd, 28 lb. of putty and 173 panes of glass from Annapolis. William Farnham also mentioned "freight of materials from Digby to Bear River" at a cost of £1,5 shillings, and three gallons of "Jamaica Spirits" used "at the raising" of the frame.

A small bill from Edward Morgan, dated March 28, 1831, charges £14, five shillings and seven pence for "hewing and hauling" 3808 feet of timber. Another account lists "two pair strong door hinges" and "one strong door lock." A Captain Morgan seemed to have been responsible for laying the foundation, as on October 14,1831, he billed the Commissioners for "underpinning" the Chapel. The Indians themselves donated the labour of digging for the foundation and clearing the land.

Towards the conclusion of the project, Judge Wiswall, writing on behalf of himself and Abbé Sigogne, praised both the Indian in charge and the general workmanship on the new church: "Through the exertions of Andrew Mewse, the Chapel at the Indian Settlement on Bear River is now well underpinned, finished and glazed on the outside, thoroughly shingled and white-washed all over so that the outside is complete. The frame is excellent and all the workmanship good, so that it may be considered a handsome and substantial building."

When commenting on the interior, Judge Wiswall stated, "the rough floor is laid on the inside and it is now fit for Divine Service." He also hoped that the inside would be "finished handsomely next year." The inside was duly finished with the uncluttered simplicity of taste that is found in many country churches. The high wainscotting of broad planks, the wide floorboards and the moulded altar, add to the pioneer atmosphere. The straight-backed pews with smoothly sculptured arms are very typical of the era.

The specifications on William Farnham's plans call for a slightly smaller building than Judge Wiswall had wanted. According to the plans, the church was to be 31 feet long by 22 feet wide and 12 feet high. The actual design of the exterior is perhaps closer to Judge Wiswall's description given on an account rendered to Farnham; Wiswall mentioned "a double door" and "a porch over the door at one end." The porch exists today, as does the double door which leads from the porch to the interior. Other design changes must have occurred as, for example, there are two windows in the gable rather than the one shown on the plan. When Farnham estimated the cost, he allowed for "a few ornaments." These materialized in the form of simple corner pilasters and returns, and straight cornice mouldings over the windows.

St. Anne's Chapel has stood on its granite block foundation for more than 150 years. It is a reminder of the faithful Abbé Sigogne and of Judge Peleg Wiswall, who learned to respect its parishioners. For all Nova Scotians, St. Anne's is a tangible part of our proud, native heritage.

St. Mary's, Lismore

If one drives along the Northumberland Strait between Pictou and Antigonish, one is following an early stagecoach route. In 1833, J. W. Blanchard ran a weekly service along the route charging passengers 20 shillings for a one-way fare. Travellers who took the trip in 1834 would have witnessed the building of one of the loveliest churches in Nova Scotia, St. Mary's Roman Catholic Church at Lismore.

There were relatively few Roman Catholic settlers in early 19th century Pictou County. The 1827 census shows that of a total population of 13,949 souls, only 1,013 were Catholics. At the time, there was no resident priest in the county. The community at Lismore, known then as Bailey's Brook, was part of the parish of Arisaig in Antigonish County. It was during the pastorate of Father William B. MacLeod that the mission church of St. Mary's was built. Father MacLeod would have been particularly interested in the area as the parish of Arisaig was his native parish. Father MacLeod was, in fact, the first son of the Diocese of Antigonish to become a priest. Years later, in 1870, when he was 72 years of age, he was appointed Vicar General of the Diocese by Bishop Colin F. MacKinnon.

Set well back from the road and sheltered by mature trees, Father MacLeod's church at Lismore is a masterpiece of pioneer architecture. No information remains about the designers or builders of St. Mary's, but the style they chose is quite clearly in the New England meeting house tradition with classical and Gothic embellishments.

The front entrance is particularly rich in classical elements. There is a superb fan light over the door, and pilasters on either side; above, there is a cornice with moulded dentil trim. The windows are of the small, muntined Gothic type. It is the original appearance of the windows that gives the church much of its authentic pioneer charm. Along each side, there are two rows of Gothic windows, with slightly smaller arches used for the top row. As well, two Gothic windows flank the main entrance, giving symmetry to the front elevation. Above the main door there is an attractive Palladian-style window with side lights; the central Gothic arch is a variation on the usual rounded classical arch of that window type.

The prototypes of this style of architecture are certainly found in the early Georgian churches built before 1830 in Nova Scotia. It is very possible that the first St. Ninian's, built in Antigonish in 1825, was the model for the builders of this church. Old photographs of St. Ninian's indicate the design was very similar with a double row of Gothic windows, a central Palladian window with a Gothic arch and a classical front entrance.

St. Mary's belfry is not original and was probably replaced in 1938 when changes were made to the interior. The square central tower was likely finished more simply with four finials and a smaller octagonal belfry like that of the early St. Ninian's. A belfry of some type existed as, in 1857, the parishioners were attempting, through the mediation of Bishop MacKinnon, to obtain church bells. Later reports indicate that at least one bell was procured.

The interior of the church is very striking. A three-sided gallery, which is reminiscent of the galleries of earlier Georgian churches, like St. Paul's in Halifax, runs along the back and down each side of the nave. The gallery is supported by square pillars which are connected by wide Gothic arches, and the gallery fronts are attractively moulded. In 1939, a new altar of North Grant stone was installed. About the same time, the old pews were also replaced. The Stations of the Cross are in memory of Margaret C. MacDonald who was Matron-in-Chief of the Canadian Nurses in World War I.

The altar is sheltered by a classical, pedimented dias with Ionic pillars. Above the dias hangs a very interesting painting of the Virgin Mary holding the Christ child on her left arm and dangling her rosary from her right hand. Her natural, almost casual, pose and the soft folds of her gown give the painting a touching realism. The congregation received the painting as a prize for their generosity. Apparently Father William B. MacLeod was a zealous promoter of higher education and encouraged his parishioners to contribute to the College at Antigonish. In 1857, his congregation at Lismore was able to give not only £46,2d in cash but 110 bushels of wheat and large quantities of other grains. Bishop MacKinnon was so pleased with the donation that he wrote of Lismore: "Their pastor has done his duty, he shall have his reward. I have a large painting of the Madonna del Rosario and I intend making a present of it to the church . . ." Thus, the beautiful piece of art, probably the work of a talented Italian painter, found its way to St. Mary's.

In spite of the difficulty of travelling in mid-19th century Nova Scotia, Bishop MacKinnon did not stint his efforts. On one trip, shortly after his consecration as Bishop in 1852, he confirmed a total of 941 candidates of seven churches located in various counties. He also crowned a newly-elected Micmac chieftan.

On June 7, 1860, he presided over the Corpus Christi celebration at Lismore. It was, in fact, the first time that St. Mary's had been chosen for the Corpus Christi procession. A newspaper account of the day tells us that "long ere the ponderous bell rang forth," the sun shone "in all his effulgent splendor" on the fields which were decked in "nature's holiday attire — the gorgeous and ever-pleasing green." When His Lordship, Bishop MacKinnon "preached an elaborate and eloquent sermon," he was heard not only by Catholics but by some interested Presbyterians! The spectacle was further enhanced by the strains of the Highland pipes and a military salute. After the Benediction, "those who carried guns fired a salute which was echoed in the distance by a piece of artillery of considerable dimensions."

The days of such colourful events and stagecoaches may be gone. But the modern traveller can still follow the old route to St. Mary's at Lismore, and admire the church our ancestors cherished so long ago.

St. Paul's, Rawdon

In 1783, Loyalist settlers came to Rawdon, in Hants County, from North and South Carolina, where they had served under Lord Rawdon during the American Revolution. One of the earliest Anglican preachers, the Rev. William Colsell King, who came in 1797, recounted to the Society for the Propagation of the Gospel in Foreign Parts that the township of Rawdon was then a wilderness about 15 miles square with about 42 families. Rev. King also noted that there was a neat little church lately erected at the expense of the government.

The little church to which Rev. King referred was the first church built at Rawdon in 1794, at a cost of £102. On March 28, 1809, the church was partially consumed by fire; although the immediate damage was fixed, the church seemed to be in constant need of repair from then on. The Rev. George W. Hill, writing in 1858, speculates that the church was probably not built properly in the first place due to the misuse of government funds. "It is impossible that justice could have been done in the first instance," he wrote, adding, "unhappily those lax views which too generally prevail at the present day in reference to work performed for the Government or the Church were even stronger than now."

In any case, when the Rev. Thomas Maynard arrived, in 1843, to find the church in a decaying condition, he resolved to build a new one. He would certainly have had the support of his congregation because he was "indefatigable in visiting and earnest in preaching" and "his whole flock were strongly and sincerely attached to him."

On March 18, 1845, Rev. Maynard chaired a special meeting of the Warden and Vestry to plan for the construction of the present St. Paul's Church. A building committee was appointed, consisting of Mr. Isaac Withrow, a member of the Vestry, and Messrs. Thomas Fenton and John Smith. It was stipulated that the "new church be erected and completed with as little delay as possible" and that it should "be built as near the South East End corner of the present burial ground as possible." It was also resolved that "the said Church shall be constructed as nearly resembling (as the Committee deemed proper) the plan submitted to this meeting by Mr. William Withrow." Mr. William Withrow was, himself, a member of the Vestry. He may have been a builder, but this is perhaps unlikely

as he was not then appointed to the building committee. More likely he had been thinking about a new church and had brought a personal sketch along to the meeting. Further resolutions also stipulated that the building should contain a vestry and that "there should be a spire attached to the new church."

In order to finance the construction of the church, a subscription list, signed by 80 families, was drawn up. The pledges totalled £125 and much of the sum was to include donated items such as shingles, lumber, and work.

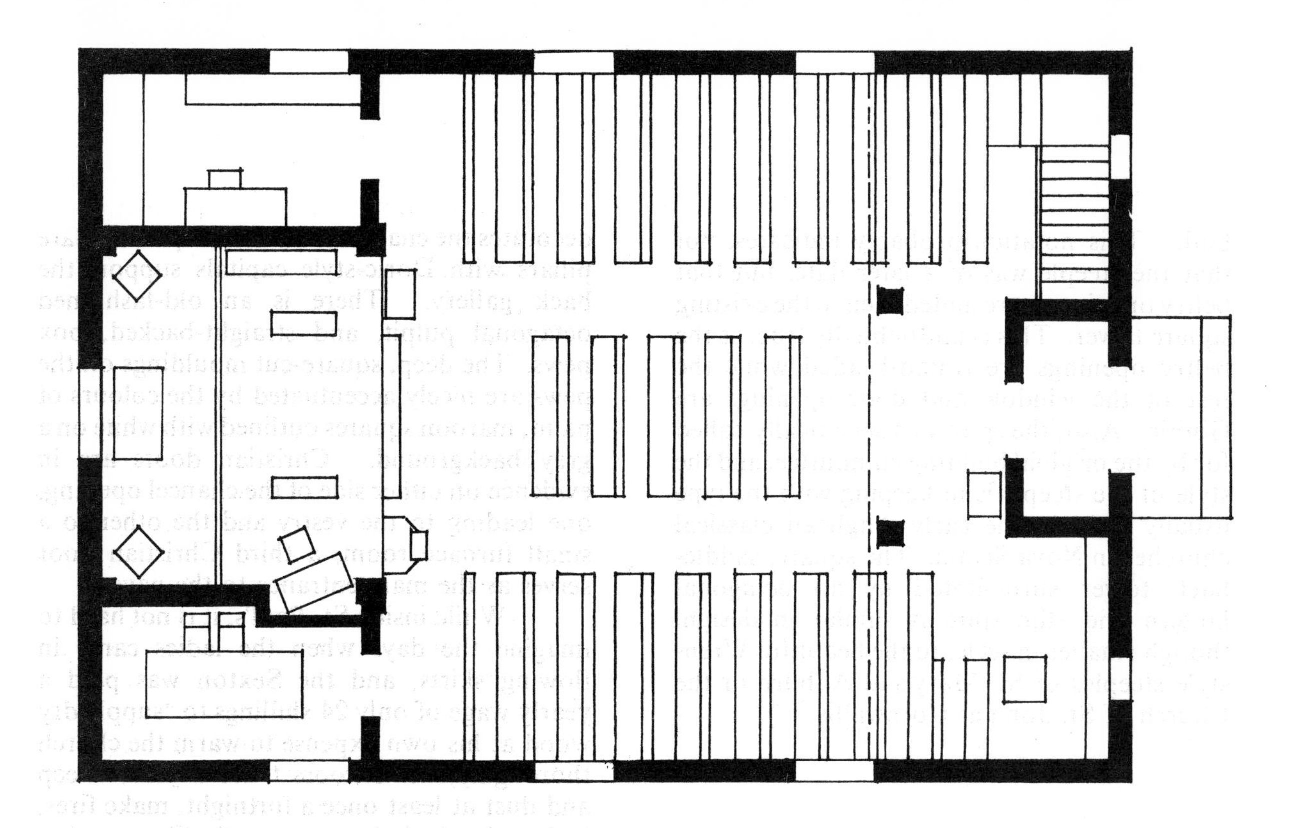

On July 29, 1845, the frame was raised, and at a special meeting less than a year later, on April 13, 1846, it was decided that the inside of the new St. Paul's was to be painted and paid for by subscription. The following year, on June 13, 1847, the church was officially consecrated by the Bishop. Shortly thereafter, the Rev. Maynard left for Digby to the great regret of his congregation who had begged him to stay longer. But having accomplished the building of a church, he probably felt he had completed a major contribution to the community.

The architectural style of St. Paul's is of the dignified, yet simple, classical variety that had been popular throughout the Georgian period. The front elevation shows the balanced symmetry, so characteristic of the classical style. The corner pilasters and returns are also typical elements of the classical mode. The windows, however, are Gothic, and the squared label moulding over the front entrance adds a touch of the English Perpendicular Gothic style.

The church records note that, in 1916, a bell was ordered from England and a belfry built. This notation probably indicates, not that the steeple was of a later date, but that belfry openings were added then to the existing square tower. This is undoubtedly true, as the belfry openings are round-headed while the rest of the window and door openings are Gothic. Also, the spire was specifically called for by the original building committee, and the style of the steeple is in keeping with the type usually used in the early Anglican classical churches in Nova Scotia. The square, saddle-back tower surmounted by an octagonal lantern and slim spire is similar in design, though smaller in scale, to the beautiful Wren-style steeples of St. Mary's at Auburn or the Church of St. John at Cornwallis.

The interior, too, is reminiscent of those earlier churches. Classical pilaster detail decorates the chancel corners, and plain square pillars with Doric-style capitals support the back gallery. There is an old-fashioned octagonal pulpit, and straight-backed, box pews. The deep, square-cut mouldings on the pews are nicely accentuated by the colours of paint, maroon squares outlined with white on a grey background. Christian doors are in evidence on either side of the chancel opening, one leading to the vestry and the other to a small furnace room; a third Christian door serves as the main entrance to the nave.

While inside St. Paul's, it is not hard to imagine the days when the ladies came in flowing skirts, and the Sexton was paid a yearly wage of only 24 shillings to "supply dry wood at his own expense to warm the church thoroughly, wash floors twice a year, sweep and dust at least once a fortnight, make fires, lock and unlock doors, cover the Communion table and care for all furniture, trim and light lamps." Outside, too, the church's lovely rural setting, high on the long range of Ardoise Hills, remains scarcely touched by modern times.

St. James', Sherbrooke

St. James' Anglican Church is a picturesque, little, white structure perched on a grassy hilltop, overlooking the St. Mary's River, in the village of Sherbrooke.

In the early days of settlement, when the main access to Sherbrooke was by water, there were no resident Anglican clergymen. However, the Colonial Church Society sent agents out to remote areas to teach and preach. In the Eastern Shore area, in 1850, Mr. Joseph Alexander was the Society's Superintending Catechist. He was not a clergyman, yet his onerous role was very close to that of a missionary.

Mr. Alexander was occupied "itinerating between nearly twenty stations to hold religious services, organize and conduct Sunday Schools, establish lending libraries, circulate Bibles, Testaments, and Tracts, and by personal visits, to carry the Gospel to the homes of the people." In his own journals, he told of the severe difficulty in going from place to place to carry out his duties. On one occasion, after performing a funeral service at Liscomb, he wrote: "After the service I returned to St. Mary's, but was nearly exhausted ere I arrived there, having to wallow through banks of snow in which I frequently sank up to the waist." On another journey, he recounted that he travelled "seven and a half hours, owing to the state of the paths."

It was during Mr. Alexander's term as Catechist on the Eastern Shore that St. James' Church was built. In an entry in his journal, dated July 20, 1850, he joyfully stated that the exterior has been completed "excepting one coat of paint to the roof." He went on to explain that the Building Committee had, that very day, settled with the contractor "after having examined the work which was passed as being highly creditable to the carpenter." Of the unfinished interior, he also noted: "A good double floor is raised, a plain reading desk, and a number of temporary seats are put up, so that services can now be held in it during the summer; and also in winter, should they be able to procure a large stove."

Mr. Alexander continued his journal entry by giving the people of Sherbrooke all the credit for building the church. While he himself attended "several of their meetings as a matter of form," he is adamant that "from first to last, it has been the people's own free will act." He concluded by saying that those who know the "long neglected locality . . . will not say, that the little Church like building, which now stands on yonder hill, built for God and His worship, is not a credit to the handful of poor Church folk here."

St. James' Church still remains a credit to its builders. Stylistically, it has the fine, simple beauty of symmetrical, classical architecture. An attractive, small fan light and classical pilaster detail decorate the front entrance. The pitched roof is graced with a square saddle-back tower, surmounted by an octagonal belfry, with rounded, classical openings and a pointed roof-spire above. The top of the weathervane has a fish design. Except for the fan light over the door, all of the

windows are Gothic; they are many-paned with old, irregular glass. A small Gothic window highlights the front gable.

The interior of the church was not properly finished until 1852. On April 2, 1852, Mr. Alexander records that he attended a meeting of the Building Committee "to devise ways and means, if possible, to finish the interior of the Church." However, the meeting adjourned shortly "as a commencement could not be made without some ready money" and until word was heard about "an application to the Society for a small grant for these purposes." The grant was forthcoming that year, and the interior duly completed.

Indeed, the interior of St. James' Church has a great deal of cosy, pioneer charm. There are box pews enclosed with doors, and an old, wood stove to heat the premises. There is an octagonal pulpit on a pedestal, of the old "wine glass" style that was popular in earlier Anglican churches of the Georgian period. Characteristically, little embellishment is in evidence, though the Gothic arch motif appears on the pew sides and doors. This motif is repeated on the pulpit and the front of the gallery which runs along the back of the church.

After the turn of the century, the church gradually deteriorated. The congregation dwindled and services were held only sporadically. Efforts were made on the upkeep of the building. Both the structure and the roof were reshingled, but some unsympathetic alterations took place in the interior. The pew doors were removed and the balcony was closed in. Fortunately, however, interest in St. James' revived in the early 1970's at the time of the major village restoration project, undertaken to make Sherbrooke the historic attraction that it is today. St. James', too, was brought back to its original condition; the pew doors were found and replaced, the gallery was opened up again, and kerosene-style lamps were installed.

During the course of restoration, a mystery arose about the date of construction of the church. The year 1840 was found to have been inscribed "on the back of one of the original shingles, on one of the boards on the

eave finish and on the south west corner post." While some felt that 1840 could have referred to the actual construction date, it is highly unlikely in the light of the carefully recorded information in Mr. Alexander's journals. Perhaps the explanation of the 1840 date is that the wood may have been recycled from another building or from an earlier attempt to build a church. A man's name, John Chisholm, was also a hidden inscription which was uncovered during restoration. Perhaps John Chisholm was the name of the carpenter who built the church, or perhaps his name, too, was on recycled wood. In any case, no firm proof about his involvement exists.

Mr. Alexander reported that on Sunday, August 15, 1852, at 5 p.m. the Bishop, who was making the first visit of any Bishop to Sherbrooke, preached "to a very attentive congregation." Not a great deal else is known about the events that took place at St. James' Church throughout the more than 100-year history. Strangely, while many baptisms occurred, only one marriage has been performed in the church; on September 8, 1945, Willena Scott wed John Simpson of Saskatchewan, a member of the Royal Canadian Air Force.

By the 1860's, the Church of England in Nova Scotia was building in the Gothic architectural style. Thus, St. James' is probably the latest existing example of an Anglican Church that was built in the style so typical of the Anglican churches in the Georgian era.

Clarence United Baptist

The United Baptist Church at Clarence is the very essence of a picturesque rural church in an idyllic pastoral setting. Sheltered by the North Mountain ridge in the Annapolis Valley, the church is situated on a secluded country road and surrounded by undulating farmland and apple orchards.

The township of Wilmot was originally settled by pre-Loyalist Planters who came in the late years of the 18th century. But Clarence itself was fairly slow to settle; by 1818, there were only 19 taxpayers located in the section. The community had no proper name until the 1850's when it was named in honour of the Duke of Clarence. However, an early church was built about 1810 and was described as having been "plain, rather longer than wide... with two doors in the east end, and the pulpit between the two entrances." As for the interior, "the pulpit was high, the pastor well shut in with doors" and "the pews were also high and fitted with doors."

No records have been found which indicate the reasons which led to the building of the new church. Most probably the membership had increased; certainly at the neighbouring Baptist church in Paradise, numbers increased dramatically from 53 persons in 1823 to 228 just ten years later. Regardless of reasons, a new church, known for many years as the North Meeting House, was erected in 1853.

This date, A.D. 1853, along with the name of the builder, C. B. Clark, were carved into the cornerstone. The information, though brief at first glance, actually provides some interesting insight into the building of churches in rural Nova Scotia.

The church is so well proportioned and has such attractive individual detailing that the modern observer might quickly assume that the structure was the creation of a highly-educated architect. Not so, however. Very few early churches were designed by architects. In this case, the builder, Charles B. Clark, was a master carpenter. He was a man of the area, having been born in Upper Granville and having married Minetta Marshall of Clarence. He had spent seven years as an apprentice and afterwards built his first house for his brother-in-law, Robert Marshall, in 1845. Eight years later, after building a number of houses in the area, he was commissioned to construct the new Baptist church. He even recycled the first church, moving it down the road for use as his carpenter shop. When Clark died in 1889, he was buried almost in sight of the church he had built.

As builder, Charles Clark would have drawn up the plans for the building and supervised the construction. He might have carried out some of the most difficult or intricate parts of the building process himself. But a great deal of the labour would likely have been carried out by others. Undoubtedly, the able-bodied men of the community would have raised the frame and helped with the construction. One writer suggested that the reason no recorded minutes of meetings about the building of the church are in existence is that the men were too busy working on it. "Not a single Conference Meeting is recorded for the year 1853," historian Margaret Leonard wrote, "and we can only suppose that the time ordinarily spent in praise and prayer of a Saturday afternoon was spent in work on the new building . . ."

The Clarence church is somewhat atypical for its time, in terms of architectural design and embellishment. For example, the plain meeting house style without a steeple was very popular with the Baptists during the 1830's, 1840's, and 1850's; such meeting houses were built as far away as Amherst Point (Cumberland County), Chebogue (Yarmouth County), or Smith's Cove (Digby County), and as close as Granville Beach and Mount Hanley in Annapolis County. And, generally, the meeting houses were much freer of embellishment, particularly forms of Gothic embellishment.

The Clarence United Baptist Church is a pleasing blend of classical and Gothic styles. The overall form is classical with the centred tower and windows placed symmetrically on either side. The door and window arches are Gothic with "eyebrow" or label mouldings, while the front gable has a classical pediment. The most eye-catching feature of the church is the open-cage belfry which combines round-headed, classical arches with decorative turned posts, and a Gothic crenellated parapet with sharp-pointed corner finials.

Between 1896 and 1905, some changes were made to the church. A vestry was added at the back of the main structure, and in order to pay for it the appropriate committee was empowered "to levy an even tax on all taxable pews as far back as the centre pillar of the gallery — pews back of that 20% less." One hundred chairs were ordered for the new vestry at a cost of 29 cents each! Also during this time the church got its first bell which necessitated some unspecified "changes in the tower." Presumably, these changes were of a relatively minor technical nature, for if the design or stylistic features had been altered, more discussion would likely have appeared in the records since a great deal of discussion about new horse sheds was recorded at that time.

Throughout the 19th century, "discipline" was observed in the Baptist church and petty crimes were often dealt with by the church. For example, if an offender stole a comb, the church would mete out a suitable punishment which could be as harsh as excommunication. At Clarence, the last record of a pastor calling for discipline was in 1895. However, no one wished to pass judgment and it was resolved: "That since we are all unworthy and probably have not shown the proper spirit toward our backsliders, every church member should consider himself the member of a committee to visit and to lend all the influence of his life to the strengthening and help of the weak and the wayward, and that it shall be the purpose of his life to lead others to a higher life."

Another custom in use during the early years of the Baptist church was the "revival."

One pastor who was particularly adept at "displays of saving power" and gaining converts was Rev. Nathaniel Vidito. It was during the ministry of Rev. Vidito that the "new" church at Clarence was built in 1853. In fact, Nathaniel Vidito was pastor at Clarence for forty years, from 1832 to 1872. He was said to have been a man of "shrewd character and pronounced convictions" who left "an abiding impression upon the people of his extensive charge."

In 1953, the Clarence United Baptist Church celebrated the 100th anniversary of the building of the church. Special services were held, historical dramas performed, and a short history written. As well, one 90-year old member of the congregation, Dr. Joel Fritz, wrote a poetic tribute.

The old church stands on this Hallowed ground
As it has stood for a hundred years.
Here good men have preached and earnestly prayed,
And the spirit sought penitent tears.

Then always with faith may the membership pray
That God, in His infinite love,
May honor you, bless, and direct you
From His home in the Heavens above.

No more fitting sentiments could be expressed now, in the church's 130th anniversary year.

St. Margaret's, Broad Cove

The 11th century Queen Margaret of Scotland, who had been a shipwrecked refugee on the shores of Scotland as a child, was raised to sainthood because of her exemplary life. She had been charitable to the poor, devoted to her faith, and committed to the building and restoration of churches. According to one biographer, her chamber "seemed to be a kind of workshop of celestial art." She was directly responsible for the building or adornment of St. Andrew's at Dumfermline and St. Margaret's Chapel on Castle Rock, Edinburgh.

It seems entirely appropriate that the Scottish Catholic pioneers from the Hebrides and Western Highlands of Scotland who came to settle on the rugged shores of Cape Breton named their fine church for Saint Margaret.

In 1825, when Bishop MacEachern of Prince Edward Island visited Broad Cove, he reported that there were 109 families, and on an earlier visit in 1823, he had noted that there was a chapel. This chapel was replaced, on a different site, by a second church which, in turn, was replaced, on yet another site, by the present edifice.

It was during the tenure of Father John Grant, the fifth resident pastor, that construction began on the new church in the summer of 1857. Father Grant was born in Pictou County in 1809, and was well known for his powerful Gaelic sermons. While it is not known who the designer or builder was, it has been reported that John MacIsaac and his cousin Big Angus MacIsaac had a sawmill at

Big River where the clapboards were sawed for the Broad Cove church. A year later, on July 8, 1858, a journalist reported on the progress of construction and financing in the Antigonish *Casket*: "The new church of St. Margaret's, Broad Cove, when terminated, will be equally creditable to the disinterested zeal of its worthy pastor and pious flock . . . Its exterior is now completely finished and . . . the sum of 750 pounds, the cost of the building is nearly paid."

The journalist also compared the design of the new church to that of the previous church: "The building is a marked improvement upon our rural church architecture. Our rude and poor imitation of Gothic spires in needle form is replaced by a neat and beautiful dome. Upon the whole, the new church of St. Margaret's at Broad Cove is an ornament to the country, and a permanent index of the religious feeling of its pastors and people."

The wide, octagonal dome and square tower with four classical pediments around the top give the church a solid, dignified aspect. The corner pilasters and returns continue the tailored dignity of impression. The long, mullioned Gothic windows add a decorative touch; the flared label mouldings are not only attractive but are one-of-a-kind. The classical rondel window in the tower is particularly ornamental with eight quatre-foil designs surrounding a central flower motif. A lacy entablature decorates the main entrance-way as well.

In 1866, the Rev. Ronald MacGillivray became the sixth resident priest at St. Margaret's. He stayed for ten years and undertook the completion of the interior of the church. Rev. MacGillivray, according to a thumbnail portrait in the February 19, 1891, issue of *The Casket*, was "a prudent, practical man of excellent counsel." However, the observer noted: "To the deserving of his flock he was a tender friend and advisor, but to the ill-behaving, his withering sarcasm was more poignant by far than the proverbial Parthian arrows."

From this description, Rev. MacGillivray is probably the sort of man who would oversee the finishing of the interior with care, not neglecting to give advice or criticism

when needed. Certainly, the interior is tastefully executed; there is a measure of practical restraint, yet embellishment enough to please the eye and lift the spirit.

The most striking feature of the interior is the three-sided gallery. It is supported by pillars with Early English-style capitals connected by wide Gothic arches. Between the arches, pilasters continue the pillar effect up to the ceiling and thus, accentuate the theatrical, sectioned appearance. In the gallery, the original straight-backed, straight-sided pews with moulded Gothic arch designs are still intact. Behind the altar, which is also original, hangs a painting of Saint Margaret wearing her

Queen's crown and humble robes. The painting is surrounded by neo-classical pillars, entablature and round-headed arch. This elaborate ornamentation is itself framed by classical columns with Ionic capitals and an imposing pediment on top.

Just as Saint Margaret built beautiful churches, so did the people of her namesake parish eight centuries later. And just as she was devout, so were they. For a small hamlet, an unusually high number of sons and daughters took up religious vocations from 1845 to 1977. Of these, three became Brothers, 29 became Sisters and 31 were ordained to the priesthood. One priest, Rev. Malcolm A. MacEachern became Bishop of Charlottetown. In view of this incredible record of devotion, it came as a shock in 1970, when it was suggested that St. Margaret's Church be closed due to a lack of priests in the diocese. The people of Broad Cove refused to accept such a devastating idea. The Bishop heard the concerns that were voiced and appointed a priest.

Many other native sons and daughters of the Broad Cove parish were successful in the fields of medicine, law, literary and cultural pursuits. For example, John L. MacDougall wrote *The History of Inverness County*, while John MacLellan was known for his Gaelic songs and poetry, and John Alexander MacIsaac became an outstanding medical doctor in the United States. A number chose political life, and one, Angus L. Macdonald, served as Premier of Nova Scotia from 1933 to 1940 and from 1945 to 1954.

May the tide of modern change leave St. Margaret's Church untouched. May the original beauty of its cladding and ornamentation remain, and may its doors stay open for its devoted congregations and its admiring visitors.

St. Andrew's, Gairloch

Saint Andrews
Presbyterian Church
Gairloch

The story of Gairloch and the building of St. Andrew's Church is filled with anecdotes of tenacity, daring, and courage that are typical of the Scottish settlers of Pictou County.

In June, 1805, two vessels, the Albatross and the Sir Sydney Smith, set sail from Stornaway, Scotland on the same day. Almost without exception, the passengers were from Gairloch, Ross-Shire, in the Highlands. Nine weeks later, the two sailing ships dropped anchor in Pictou harbour within ten minutes of each other. Of the new arrivals, the MacKenzies, MacPhersons, MacDonalds, Sutherlands, and Fergusons settled a tract of land, between West and Middle Rivers, which they named after their native home.

There were many hardships for the new settlers. Firstly, they had to carry all of their cooking utensils, food, and farm implements on their backs as they walked the 20 miles from Pictou to Gairloch. There was often a shortage of food; one spring they had to walk as far as Truro to get seed potatoes, and another time, some of the newly-planted potato splits had to be hurriedly dug up and eaten.

The native tongue of those early settlers of Gairloch was Gaelic, and to this day, their descendants speak with a strong Scottish brogue. Their religion was Presbyterian and most were loyal to the Church of Scotland. There were a few "Antiburghers," whose brand of Presbyterianism did not favour the established church. Traditionally, those that were solidly for the Church of Scotland were also solidly Conservative in politics, while the Antiburgher faction was Liberal. The 1862 election bore this division out. The Gairloch vote was 120 Conservatives and 4 Liberals, and it was noted that if the schoolmaster had stayed home, the Liberal vote would have been 3.

Nineteenth century Gairlochers were god-fearing folk who read the Bible and prayed, usually on their knees, twice daily. They attended church diligently, the ladies taking great care over a boiling, iron tea kettle to steam the wrinkles out of the veils on their bonnets for the occasion. Sometime between 1816 and 1822, an early church was built on a lot of land adjoining the site of the present church. An important annual event was the celebration of the Lord's Supper during the summer. People from all over the county gathered for six days of services. The Gaelic services were held outside near the entrance to the present cemetery. For this event, a temporary wooden structure called the "Tent" was built to shelter the minister.

At a meeting of the congregation on January 2, 1855, it was decided that a new church would be built. Three members were designated to form a building committee, and it was further resolved that the exterior of the new church be completed on or before November 1, 1856. Thus, the speed of construction was an important factor, as was the size of the new edifice. There is a story that three men (probably the building committee) travelled on horseback to Pictou and New Glasgow in order to measure the newest churches, so that they might return to Gairloch and build a church one foot longer and one foot wider than any in the county.

The new church was built quickly, if not exactly on time. For, at a meeting on August 30, 1858, a visiting clergyman congratulated those present "on having finished the church in so good and neat a manner." The building was a large size too, measuring 46 feet in width by 76 feet in length. It was completed at a total cost of £1494 and 13 shillings. Of this sum, the cost of the frame and related materials was approximately £174 and the masonry for the foundation amounted to about £90. Substantial sums were also paid to the joiners, Malcolm McDonald and Morrison & Brown Company. Donald Fraser, the plasterer, also received remuneration as did Alex Gillis, the painter. Numerous firms and individuals were paid for unspecified services or tasks during the construction of the building. It is not noted who drew up the plans for the new church. But a small sum of money, seven shillings and six pence, was paid to Donald Grant of New Glasgow. Grant was a young builder of the Church of Scotland persuasion. It is known that he was involved in the building of the Kirk Church in New Glasgow about the same time, and that he became the builder of the MacLennan's Mountain church two years later in 1860. It is quite possible that he contributed the plans for the Gairloch church as well.

Funds were raised to pay for the new church by the sale of pews to the families which made up the congregation. A total of 126 pews were sold to the people of Gairloch and the neighbouring communities such as Mill Brook, Lairg, and Middle River. The congregation was certainly substantial, for on March 5, 1864, it was recorded that the average church attendance was 800 strong.

Indeed, Gairloch itself was a flourishing and self-sufficient community in the 19th century. There were three stores, a tannery run by Hector MacKenzie, and woodworking shop where Donald MacPherson made furniture. At one time, there were no less than eight blacksmiths' shops where "the sound of the hammer on the anvil and the smell of burning hooves" were familiar sounds and scents for six days of the week.

As well, there was a cheese factory, known as the Central Cheese Company of Gairloch, which operated in the 1870's and 1880's. The cheese factory was centrally located next to the church; its second floor was the scene for many a "pie social" on a winter's evening when the community entertained itself with songs and recitations. The factory must have been very productive and prosperous, for on Christmas Eve in 1880, three men of Gairloch delivered a gift of one day's output of cheese to the manse. When the Rev. Neil Brodie returned home late that evening, his surprise and gratitude were unbounded upon seeing "so great a mountain of cheese." There were four large cheeses in all, weighing a total of 200 pounds!

Like any thriving church, St. Andrew's had its share of famous sons. Perhaps the most notable are George Munro and Colonel Lawrence Howard MacKenzie. George Munro was born in 1825, and learned about the business of printing in Pictou at the early age of twelve. By 1856, he worked for a New York publisher, and soon owned his own company which successfully mass-produced good literature. He was a great benefactor of Dalhousie University, saving the institution from ruin in 1879 and twice subsequently.

Colonel Lawrence Howard MacKenzie was born in 1876 and distinguished himself as a military man. At the outbreak of the first World War, he was promoted to the rank of Major. By 1918, he was sent two hundred miles within the Arctic Circle in North Russia to combat the Bolshevik attacks. He commanded a group of international soldiers which made a three-day march through the Arctic snows and winds and captured Segeja on February 19, 1919. He was awarded the Distinguished Service Order for "his sound judgment and his courage." He also received the Croix de Guerre from France, the Order of St. Anne from Russia, and the Royal Order of the White Eagle with Swords from Serbia.

Through the years, St. Andrew's has had a long line of interesting and stalwart ministers. For example, the youthful and spirited Rev. Thomas Irving served from 1899 to 1904. After moving into the manse, he married a local girl, and began to organize Sunday schools in Gairloch and two neighbouring communities. The Rev. Neil Brodie, who was a bachelor from Scotland, ministered to Gairloch from 1868 to 1876, and was then brought back, because of his popularity, from 1880 to 1886. More recently, Rev. Donald C. MacDonald, a native of

Pictou County and minister at Gairloch from 1942 to the end of 1943, was named moderator of the Presbyterian Church of Canada on June 5, 1983.

Today, much has changed in Gairloch. Like many rural communities it is no longer self-sufficient and bustling with activity. The local industries have disappeared or moved into the towns and cities. Many of the farms that once prospered are now overgrown with forests. Gairloch is a quiet settlement, a scattering of farms along a country road. The church remains as a landmark and a fitting legacy from a glorious past.

The church is classical in style and detail, with the exception of the Gothic arches of the windows, the central doorway, and belfry openings. Classical simplicity and symmetry are evident in the front elevation where the entrance is flanked by a single window on each side. Classical pilaster detailing and returns decorate the corners of the structure. The long, Gothic windows are mullioned and delicately outlined by label mouldings.

Above the central gable sits the square saddleback belfry tower. Originally, four finials graced the tower, where, today, a peaked roof caps it off. The change was made in the early years of this century. Two entries in the minute book for 1906 indicate that repairs were made to the belfry tower that summer, and old photographs show that the peaked roof had certainly been added before 1911. Undoubtedly, the new roof, while not as decorative as the finials, was very practical and probably less prone to leaks.

While the exterior of the church is pleasing in its traditional design, it is the interior which is striking in classical beauty and pioneer charm. The pews are of the old-fashioned, box style, enclosed by doors. There are spacious galleries on three sides of the church, each containing three more rows of box pews. The galleries are supported by solid rounded columns with Doric capitals. Everywhere there is decorative moulding — on the pew doors, along the fronts of the galleries, and on the interior doors. For example, the door to the session room which leads off the foyer has reeded side trim and a classical pediment above. The impressive, high pulpit is accented by detailed moulding and sturdy round side pillars which give it a strong, fortified appearance. The podium below the pulpit was once occupied by both an English and a Gaelic precentor who "gave the line" or intoned the psalms, line by line, for the congregation to follow.

The interior is painted in bright, fresh pastel colours with white trim, and is completely free of any signs of deterioration. The present congregation should be proud that there is not a crack to be seen. Indeed, the feeling of 'newness' swiftly transports the visitor's imagination back to the early years of the church's history. Somehow, one would not be at all surprised to see hundreds of ladies in long skirts and bonnets and menfolk in their Sunday best thronging into the large church and filling up the pews. What a sight to see! What a treasure the Gairloch church is of those halcyon days!

St. Matthew's, Halifax

The congregation of St. Matthew's United Church, on Barrington Street in Halifax, is the oldest dissenting congregation in Canada. Initially, the Dissenters, Congregationalists and Presbyterians, attended services at St. Paul's Anglican Church which opened in 1750, shortly after the founding of Halifax. When Rev. Aaron Cleveland arrived to minister to the dissenting flock, he preached at St. Paul's on Sunday afternoons. He was said to have been "a popular and engaging preacher" who often drew a number of Anglicans to his afternoon services.

The City's founder, Colonel Edward Cornwallis, assigned a lot of land for the building of the first Dissenters Meeting House at the southwest corner of Prince and Hollis streets. The meeting house, known at first as Mathers, served its congregation, which gradually became more Presbyterian as some Congregationalists returned to New England. Eventually Presbyterian ministers were called. On New Year's Day of 1857, a fire swept Hollis Street and the old Mather's Church was lost. Subsequently, a new site was chosen on Pleasant Street (now Barrington) in the fashionable southern suburb beside the Governor's house.

The building of the present St. Matthew's Church was not without vicissitudes. On May 28, 1857, the Building Committee reviewed proposed drawings submitted by two architects, Mr. David Stirling and Mr. Cyrus Pole Thomas; the Committee unanimously accepted Mr. Thomas' concept which resembled his design for St. Andrew's Church in Hamilton. Cyrus Thomas was also responsible for the magnificent Old Court House on Spring Garden Road and would, after 1859, become the designer of the Italianate Granville Street buildings. He was one of the sons of William Thomas, head of the prestigious architectural firm of William Thomas & Sons of Toronto.

In late September of that year, tenders were called for a building to be built of freestone according to Cyrus Thomas' plans. Unfortunately, only two offers were received and both were too costly. At their November 16, 1857 meeting the Building Committee resolved that £8,000 was the upper limit of their funds to build the church. Since Mr. Thomas' plans could not be carried out for this sum, they were subsequently abandoned, and he was asked to prepare new drawings altogether. By March of 1858 a second set of drawings had been received from Cyrus Thomas, and tenders were again called for. This time the church was to be constructed of rough brick covered with mastic with a freestone front. Evidently further cutbacks became necessary, as the church was ultimately built entirely of brick.

Three tenders, all of which were in excess of £8,000, were received. The Building Committee wrote to Thomas' firm explaining that none of the bids could be accepted. Fortunately, a few days later, one of the contractors, the firm of Peters, Blaiklock and

Peters, which had probably heard of the difficulties, offered to make a donation of £243. This, in effect, reduced the bid to £8,232, which was finally accepted by the Committee. A footnote to the difficulties of trying to keep the costs down is that before construction was completed, the total figure had escalated to more than £12,000.

At 11 o'clock in the morning on June 18, 1858, the cornerstone was laid by the Hon. James McNab "in the presence of a large and respectable concourse of citizenery of all denominations." A scroll containing the history of the church as well as the names of the architect's firm, contractors, subscribers and church officials was deposited in the cornerstone along with newspapers, coins and Belcher's Almanack.

Construction must have progressed well, as on November 8, 1858, a report in *The Morning Sun* noted "the rafters are now being set up and we expect in a short time to see the whole roof closed in." The report also hinted at some of the finishing details: "We believe it is intended to place stained glass in the large circular window in the rear — this will doubtless have a very fine effect in the interior of the church."

The following year, on May 20, 1859, the same newspaper stated that the brick church was "rapidly drawing to completion" and would be "quite an ornament to that part of the city." Three months later, on August 9, 1859, *The British Colonist* reported, "the Union Jack was hoisted on the spire of the new church" and "three cheers were given by the men employed." The workmen, under the direction of Mr. Cornelius Phalen, had just completed the difficult task of "tinning" the roof of the spire.

St. Matthew's is an excellent example of restrained, Mid-Victorian Gothic architecture. The configuration is still symmetrical and the Gothic detailing is not exaggerated. Most of the exterior embellishment is found on the bell tower. In the centre of the tower there is a large Gothic window with a flower motif in the point of the arch. Higher up, the belfry openings are paired Gothic arches with carved label mouldings. The belfry has a crenellated top accented with four large finials at the corners and smaller finials in between; the unadorned spire rises above this ornamented parapet.

Further Gothic touches are achieved by the diagonal corner buttress on the tower and on the main structure where they are finished by high carved finials. Along the side elevations, Gothic windows and buttresses alternate.

Fewer Gothic elements than might be expected exist in the interior, which is very reminiscent of classical pioneer churches of the Georgian era. One finds old-style box pews with doors and a high, richly decorated pulpit with a sweep of stairs leading up to it on either side. There is an open, three-sided gallery supported by round pillars with round moulded capitals and extremely attractive, carved brackets. The flower-like motifs on the brackets and the moulding on the decorative gallery fronts are highlighted by shades of blue and gold paint on a white background.

On the back wall, above the pulpit, cradled in the arms of a Gothic arch, is a magnificent rose window. The window, a replica of one in the cathedral at Chartres, France, has a central flower surrounded by a whorl of 12 large petals and an outer ring of 12 small flowers. The multi-coloured stained glass is predominantly blue and gold, and adds an unusually beautiful jewel-like glitter to the interior of the church.

St. Matthew's has undergone relatively few changes over the years. In 1892, the plaster ceiling of the interior was sheathed in wood, and one year later, a vicious storm damaged the roof and spire which had to be partly rebuilt. In 1917, the Halifax Explosion, caused by the collision of the munitions ship *Mont Blanc* with the *Imo* in the Halifax harbour, resulted in $4,000 worth of damage to St. Matthew's windows and organ. In 1945, the explosion in the Bedford Magazine shattered the large Gothic window in the steeple which was repaired at a cost of $2,300.

Many interesting ministers have served the congregation over the years. Rev. John Scott of Jedburgh, Scotland, who served the longest term, from 1826 to 1863, was in charge when the present church was built. Following Rev. Scott was Rev. Dr. George Munro Grant, a most distinguished Canadian. Born in Albion Mines, Nova Scotia, Grant was educated at the Pictou Academy and the University of Glasgow in Scotland. In 1873, while still minister of St. Matthew's, he wrote *Ocean to Ocean*, a book about his travels in Western Canada with Sir Sanford Fleming. In 1877, George Munro Grant left St. Matthew's to become principal of Queen's University in Kingston, Ontario.

Considering St. Matthew's ecumenical beginnings it is hardly surprising that, in 1925, the congregation joined the United Church of Canada. Today, St. Matthew's stands across from the pioneer cemetery at a busy modern intersection. The church is a proud symbol of its early roots and of the good taste and sense of style of its builders.

St. John's,
MacLennan's Mountain

Today, if one sets out to find MacLennan's Mountain, it is not easy. On leaving Stellarton, signs for McLellan's Brook and McLellan's Mountain must be followed, for the original name of MacLennan's Mountain is no longer used on modern road maps and signs. It is only when one leaves the pavement altogether, travels down a gravel road taking an unmarked fork which leads along a much narrower, rutted and winding road, that one finally reaches the destination. At last, there is no mistaking either the place or the church. The structure is staunchly perched on a high, cleared knoll, and the words "ST. JOHN'S PRESBYTERIAN CHURCH, MACLENNAN'S MOUNTAIN, ERECTED 1860" are boldly printed on a plaque above the main door.

It was to this almost hidden rural setting that the Rev. Donald Allan Fraser came in 1817. A native of Argyleshire, Scotland, Rev. Fraser was the first minister of the established Church of Scotland to come to Nova Scotia. Earlier preachers to come to the province had been associated with the Antiburgher faction of Presbyterianism. It was in direct response to the appeals of the Church of Scotland settlers, many of whom were highlanders who spoke only Gaelic, that Rev. Donald Allan Fraser came.

Rev. Fraser was described as being "full of Highland fervor, young and of prepossessing appearance, an accomplished scholar and powerful Gaelic speaker." The congregation he came to at MacLennan's Mountain consisted of about 40 families who had been part of an early Highland emigration to Pictou County. Indeed, the earliest settlers to the county were from the Highlands of Scotland. It is curious that the first systematic attempt at settlement in Pictou County was due to American enterprise. The Philadelphia Land Company received a grant from the British government of 100,000 acres, encompassing most of Pictou County and part of Colchester County. Many families came out from the old country under the auspices of this company.

It is no wonder that, with his physical and intellectual qualities, Rev. Fraser ministered with great energy and success for 21 years. The congregation greatly regretted his departure for Lunenburg in 1838.

Rev. Alexander McGillivray who had been preaching at Barney's River and Merigomish was then called to MacLennan's Mountain where he spent the remaining 24 years of his life. McGillivray had been born in Invernesshire, Scotland, in 1801; he had come to Nova Scotia immediately following his ordination in April, 1832.

Rev. McGillivray was a peace-loving man and refused to take part in any of the bitter verbal disputes with the Antiburgher clergy as his predeccessor had so aptly done. One of the leading members of his flock, Squire John MacKay, recounted this trait with some regret, "Although a good man, he was not fitted for contention. He shrank from it." But when great difficulties arose in the Church of

Scotland, Alexander McGillivray showed almost superhuman bravery and perseverance.

In 1843, a second secession or Disruption took place in the Church of Scotland in its homeland. Of the 1203 ministers, 451 seceded to form the Free Church. In Pictou County, secession occurred too, but on a much small scale, and for the most part, the highlanders remained faithful to the Church of Scotland. In spite of this fidelity, seven of the eight Church of Scotland ministers left to go back to the old country to fill vacant positions there. Rev. McGillivray was the only one to stay and care for all of the Church of Scotland congregations in the county. Even a strong appeal from his colleague, Rev. R. Williamson, did not change his mind. "I adjure you to follow," wrote Williamson, ". . . . preparation is made for your appointment.... Don't worry yourself with ideas of remote stations and poor livings of £150 or £120 a year.... Most horrid and gloomy must be the prospect of remaining there be." Yet, McGillivray remained, steadfastly preaching throughout Pictou County to his many flocks for nine long years.

Preaching to the settlers of mid-19th century Nova Scotia must have been extremely exhausting. For it was not merely a matter of preaching to the assembled once or twice on a Sunday, but it was usually a four-day speaking event at each place. In December, 1849, the *Edinburgh Christian Magazine* published an article, written by Dr. McNair, on Alexander McGillivray's labours in Pictou County. McNair, who visited Pictou County, gives an account of services at MacLennan's Mountain, where there was "an immense gathering" of people who came "on foot or in gigs or wagons, jolting over breakneck corduroy roads . . . ." McGillivray, he said, "was the sole Gaelic labourer . . . . and yet the old soldier will rather spend and be spent in the service of his master than that the people should be sent empty away." Another story is told of Rev. McGillivray that, after baptizing 22 children in one day at Gairloch, he heard, while travelling home, that one of his own sons had been born that day. He was so anxious to return that he and his horse swam perilously across the swollen East River which was in spring flood and considered impassable.

Help finally came in 1853, when three young ministers arrived from Scotland.

McGillivray, himself, had also taken steps to secure the future of the clergy in Pictou County by sending four young Pictonians over to Scotland to be educated for the ministry.

In 1858, Queen's University, in Kingston, Ontario, conferred the degree of Doctor of Divinity upon Rev. McGillivray. About that time, too, his MacLennan's Mountain congregation decided that a new and larger church was needed. Builder Donald Grant of New Glasgow supervised the construction of the new church. Both labour and materials were contributed by members of the congregation. In 1860, at a total cost of £650, St. John's was completed. The seating capacity was about 600. It is unlikely that the congregation ever grew to that extent. In 1875, there were 160 families in the congregation with 195 communicants, but by 1913, the numbers had dwindled to only 75 families.

The church that New Glasgow's Donald Grant and the MacLennan's Mountain congregation built is of particular interest because it typifies the most popular architectural style used for Presbyterian church buildings in mid-19th century rural Pictou County.

The popular style is a simple rectangular meeting house with no steeple. The cladding is clapboard, and the windows are elongated rectangles with simple mouldings over the tops. A small window, often a rondel window, decorates the front gable. In the case of St. John's, the gable window was originally round and, hopefully, will be restored to that design again. There are classical touches, such as the moulded corner pilasters and returns which add elegance to the fairly severe style. The central doorway is very eye-catching. It, too, looks elongated, as there is a large moulded panel above the actual entrance; this panel serves to extend the height of the doorway to that of the two windows on either side.

The interior of St. John's gives the visitor a definite and almost tangible feeling of the past. There are the old box pews with the small doors to enclose them. And best of all, there is a very high, 'fire and brimstone' pulpit which is built with heavy, moulded pillars at each corner. On each side of the pulpit, a curving staircase heads up to the door which, when unlatched, admits one to the high position. There is a three-sided balcony, supported by solid round pillars with Doric capitals; in recent years, the balcony area has been closed in to create a Sunday school area. The balcony fronts, which are still in place, are attractively moulded, as are the pew doors and the two aisle doors which lead into the main body of the church. The moulded woodwork is accentuated by the contrasting colours of light beige paint and the darker brown of wood-graining which are used throughout.

On Christmas Eve of 1860, Dr. McGillivray preached at the official opening of his fine new church. A little more than one year later, on February 16, 1862, he died at 61 years of age. An impressive, "cathedral-shaped" monument of native stone was placed in front of the church by his grateful followers. One of the white marble plaques on the monument attests to Dr. McGillivray's "Evangelical simplicity and his untiring fortitude during a long period of spiritual destitution in the mission field of Nova Scotia."

Dr. McGillivray's church also embodies simplicity and fortitude which have stood the test of time. It has survived the philosophical divisions within the church and the wintry blasts which have raged about its unprotected hilltop position for more than 100 years. In 1976, the church survived a cruel and mindless attack by vandals. The necessary repairs were made, so that the Mountain Church, as it is affectionately called, may continue to give pleasure to all who appreciate its history and its beauty.

St. Ninian's Cathedral, Antigonish

The history of St. Ninian's Cathedral in Antigonish dates back to the early days of the settlement. Initially, a number of British officers and soldiers, under Colonel Heirlihy, arrived at Antigonish Harbour in 1784. The small settlement grew slowly at first, and was known alternately as Dorchester or Antigonish, a Micmac Indian word meaning "a forked river of fish." In 1810, the first Roman Catholic chapel was built, and by 1824, a second, wooden St. Ninian's was constructed on Main Street.

During the next forty years, the parish grew steadily. St. Francis Xavier College which had been founded by Bishop Colin F. MacKinnon in Arichat was moved to Antigonish in 1855. The College flourished, serving the educational needs of the predominantly Roman Catholic Scottish population. By 1866, the College was granted full university status. About the same time, Bishop MacKinnon's vision of a great stone cathedral had begun to take shape.

The Bishop suggested the idea of a new stone edifice to his parishioners, and they accepted the challenge eagerly, pledging an annual total of £900, and volunteering three days of labour each week with the exception of harvest season. On October 22, 1866, Bishop MacKinnon turned the first sod on the new site chosen for the church, a high point of land overlooking the town.

Shortly after Christmas, the parishioners began the arduous job of hauling stone, by horse and wagon, to the construction site. Fortunately, large quantities of stone were available within four miles of the town. The limestone, required for the foundation and walls of the church, came from MacAdam quarry at Brierly Brook while the freestone or sandstone for the trim came from Arsenault quarry at North Grant. Stones weighing four to eight hundred pounds were not unusual, and some weighed as much as two tons each. A timely shipwreck at Morristown, in Antigonish Harbour, also helped the project along. The cargo of lumber was procured at a bargain price and quickly transported across the ice by the parishioners and their sleighs.

On May 16, 1867, Bishop MacKinnon and the resident pastor, Father Hugh Gillis, hired a master stonemason, Ronald MacGillivray of Hallowell Grant, to lay the foundation. Accordingly, trenches were dug around the perimeter, and foundation walls, 43 inches thick, were constructed. There was to be no basement beneath the main body of the church which was supported on square stone posts about 40 inches wide and 80 inches deep. Massive hand-hewn beams were than placed on top of the supporting posts and the floor boards were laid, in turn, on top of the beams.

Ronald MacGillivray, under the direction of the dedicated Father Hugh Gillis, completed his task in good time. Less than six weeks later, on June 29, 1867, two days prior to Confederation, the cornerstone was laid by Very Reverend Dr. John Cameron, Vicar General of the Diocese.

Bishop MacKinnon selected the architectural plans for the cathedral. He rejected the first set of plans, prepared by an eminent local architect, Owen Hammill on the grounds that they were too extravagant. A second set of plans, submitted by a Montreal architect. A. Leveque, met with the wise Bishop's approval. Hamill was, however, involved in the project, for a notice in the *Colonial Standard* of June 4, 1867, announced that he had removed from Pictou to Antigonish where he would remain until the completion of St. Ninian's. Presumably, he interpreted the plans and specifications of the out-of-town architect for the local workmen. The master builder for the cathedral was Sylvester O'Donoghue, a native of Coolruss, County Wicklow in Ireland. At the time of this commission, he was 29 years old and had just completed work on a Halifax church.

By August of 1874, seven years after the cornerstone had been laid, Bishop MacKinnon's dream was a reality. The interior plastering was nearing completion, and four new bells, cast in Dublin, had been suspended in the western tower. The original bell from the old wooden St. Ninian's was transferred to its lofty position in the eastern tower.

On September 13, 1874, St. Ninian's was officially opened and dedicated. The day had dawned clear and bright for the several thousand visitors that thronged to the ceremony. One eyewitness described the scene: "Towards the hour of service in the church it grew quite warm and the sky was gloriously blue and flecked with pieces of cloud and the breeze was an autumnal benediction. From an early hour there had been motion among the people, and the rattle of carriages disturbed the slumbers of those to whom early hours are at once unfriendly and unfamiliar. Soon the carriages began to increase and before nine o'clock strings of them came along the various roads leading into the town, all containing persons to witness the dedicatory services." The ceremony must have been impressive with no less than five bishops in attendance, along with the Vicar General of the diocese, Archbishop Connolly of Halifax and some fifty priests. And the parishioners must have been duly proud when Archbishop Connolly praised their efforts. "The building of a temple to the Almighty," he said, "was the noblest of Christian works. All other works were of the earth. They rendered no glory to Heaven and little or no lasting credit to those who created them. But the highest effort of greatness, the most lavish expenditure of wealth, the most generous sacrifices on the part of the people— all was best made and exerted in the one great act of building a temple to the Most High."

The completed edifice, which cost £40,000, measured 170 feet in length and 70 feet in width and had a seating capacity of 1500. The overall impression of the cathedral, at first glance, is one of solidity and dignity. The style is Romanesque, with a row of nine round-headed windows along each side accented by a row of nine rondel windows above. Two impressive square towers, each 125

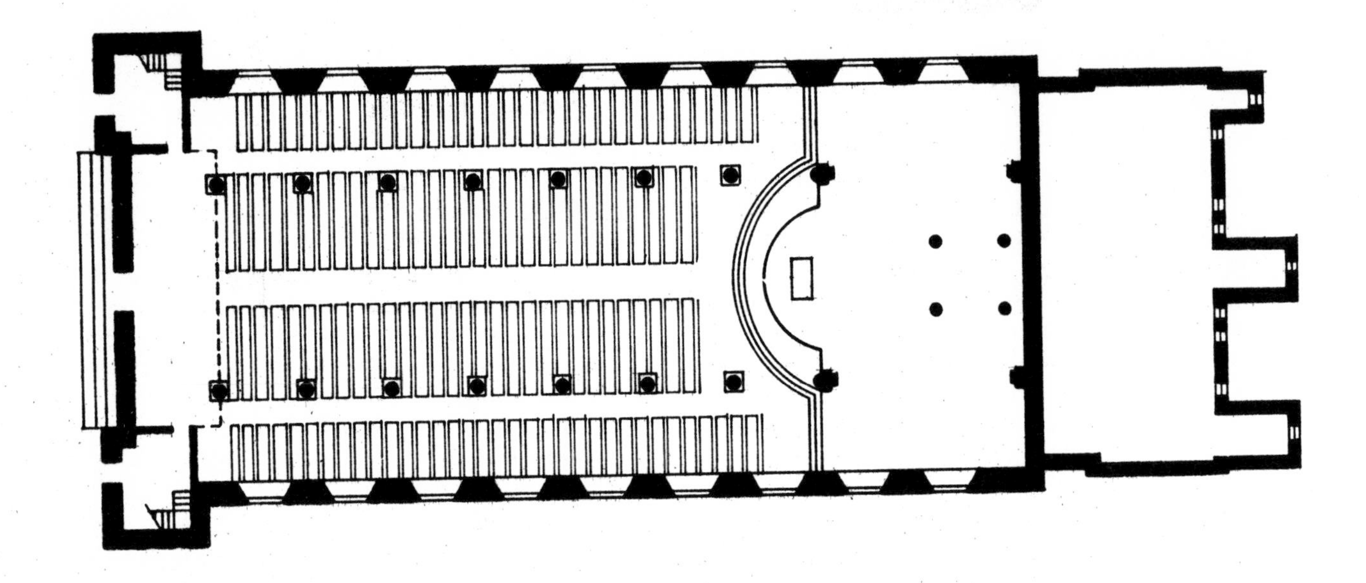

feet high, flank the front entrance. The towers have semi-circular, louvred belfry openings, and are elegantly finished by round domes surmounted by octagonal lanterns, each topped with a cross.

Between the towers, the 100-foot front façade of Baroque style adds an unexpected touch of flamboyance to the sedate dignity of the structure. The façade is embellished with arched niches and carved scrollwork, and rises to a central Baroque pediment. Two Gaelic words, "Tigh Dhe" or House of God, were boldly emblazoned there by stone cutter McIsaac of Dunmore. The main entrance is decorated with a keystone arch, side pilasters and a classical pediment above. On either side of the doorway, the armorial crests of Bishop MacKinnon and Pope Pius IX were carved into the façade. Also immortalized in stone, above the grand central portal, are a humble cluster of shamrocks and two sprigs of thistle, probably in honour of the church's Irish builder and the Scottish ancestry of the parishioners.

The interior with its lofty, frescoed ceiling, is immediately pleasing to the eye. The high, arched windows are of etched glass decorated with small stained glass panes bearing Biblical symbols such as the Cross, the Ark or the Dove. The most striking features of the interior are the magnificent colonnades along each side of the nave. Graceful Romanesque arches supported by seven slender pillars with richly ornamented Corinthian capitals, create a visual rhythm and well-ordered beauty. Indeed, the composition of the interior is reminiscent of San Spirito, an Italian Renaissance basilica in Florence which was designed by the celebrated Filippo Brunelleschi in 1436. This similarity is not entirely surprising as Bishop MacKinnon, who had comissioned the building of St. Ninian's, had spent nine years in Italy and must have been familiar with the great Renaissance basilicas. But St. Ninian's is not as elaborate as San Spirito and produces a simpler and more unified effect on the visitor. One travelling journalist described his impressions clearly: "On entering the church, the first thing that strikes one is its intense purity . . . a purity of style and ornamentation, a purity of meaning in the interior which, even apart from the sacred character of the building, would impressively affect a stranger."

The frescoes were begun in 1899 by Ozias LeDuc, a Quebec artist who had been trained in Paris. On the ceiling, four large circular paintings depict the Nativity, the Crucifixion, the Ascension, and Christ as the Good Shepherd. Above the arches are the standing figures of the Apostles and a few early saints. A large oil painting of St. Ninian, done in 1857 by the Italian artist, Appollonio, was transferred to the Cathedral from the earlier church.

Alterations to the cathedral occurred in 1937. A small stone addition comprising a sacristy, vestry and offices was attached behind the sanctuary or chancel. In order to facilitate this change, the Romanesque chancel window was removed and blocked in; three panels of the window were then relocated behind the side altars along with a new fourth panel to balance the set. The side wings of the sanctuary were opened up to the view of the main body of the church by means of arches. A new altar of North Grant stone was set under an ornate canopy supported by four pillars. Architect for the stuctural changes was A.W. Holmes of Toronto while the sanctuary décor was carried out by the Robert Couseland Company of Toronto. Further alterations were carried out in 1957 when a new floor was laid, new pews installed and a new heating system incorporated in the church. At this time, a number of the frescoes were restored. More recently, for the centennial celebrations, the sanctuary was again altered with the widening of the steps leading into the sanctuary and the elevation of the altar to increase the space and visibility for the ceremonies.

It is fitting that the stately cathedral is named after St. Ninian, a fifth century Briton who had founded Christianity in Scotland and who had himself "built a church of stone."

TIGH DHE.

Fort Massey, Halifax

Fort Massey United Church, at the corner of Queen and Tobin streets in Halifax, has an unique name which recalls the early days of the garrison town. In 1777, an outpost fort was established on a hill to the south of the Citadel in order to prevent an attack from that direction. The fort, which consisted of earthworks and an octagonal blockhouse which could accommodate 30 soldiers, was named after General Eyre Massey, its commanding officer.

In 1815, the fort was dismantled, and the town gradually expanded southward. Streets were laid out and houses built. By 1868, two of the town's Presbyterian churches, Poplar Grove and Chalmers, decided to open a Sunday School in the area. The success of Fort Massey District Sunday School was soon acknowledged and a group of members from the two churches asked the presbytery to establish Fort Massey Church.

On June 25, 1870, the cornerstone was laid with appropriate ceremony. William Garvie, a founding editor of *The Citizen* and Commissioner of Mines in the provincial government, read the scroll that was placed in the cavity of the stone. The Hon. William J. Stairs, prominent financier and politician, pronounced the stone "well and truly laid."

Contractor for the new church was John Brookfield, and upon his death, his son Samuel completed the work. The total cost of construction was $42,000 of which $17,000 had been initially raised by subscription. The project, which was a major building task,

progressed quickly. Just one year and a halt later on December 10, 1871, Fort Massey was opened for Divine Worship.

In order to select the most suitable design, an architectural competition had been held and the plans of David Stirling chosen. Stirling was a well-known Halifax architect who had designed the Halifax Club in 1862 and the Grafton Street Methodist Church (now St. David's) in 1866. In 1873, the *Canadian Illustrated News* praised Fort Massey Church as "one of the most handsome specimens of Gothic architecture to be met in the Dominion."

Fort Massey is the very essence of Gothic styling. The main structure is built of a light, red-gold brick with an ironstone foundation; the handsome detailing was fashioned in red sandstone by John Sheriff. The massive, carved portal has three pillared entrance arches with decorated, gabled tops. Above the portal is a pair of large Gothic windows with carved surrounds and ornate geometrical tracery. The central gable above the windows is graced with a round, ornamental window with its own tracery design. Indeed, there are at least 25 varieties of decorative tracery in more than a half dozen different window shapes, all in the Gothic tradition.

The steeple, at the southwest shoulder of the building, displays a combination of different window sizes at each stage. The lowest stage has a pair of small lancet arches, the second stage has a single, larger window arch topped with a carved stone gable, and the topmost portion contains a small, single lancet beneath the bracketed flare of the spire. Large stone finials, one short and one tall, and buttresses finish the opposite front corner of the church.

The *Halifax Reporter* once noted: "the interior has a rich and pleasing effect and with a multitude of pillars, corbels, capitals and arches has almost a cathedral appearance. In form and style there is nothing similar to it in Nova Scotia." Fort Massey is said to be the first Presbyterian Church to use the cruciform plan with a nave, side aisles and transepts. From within, it is easy to see the overall plan at a glance. It is also in the interior that the remarkable variety of windows makes its greatest impression. The high clerestory windows, that send shafts of light down into the nave, are small, single arches with tracery in a trefoil design. Along the side aisles are wider, three-sectioned windows with trefoil tracery, and each transept has one large round and two long Gothic windows, all with intricate tracery.

The interior contains a great many tasteful examples of Gothic embellishment. The richly carved ceiling braces are completed by prominent hammer-beams which, in turn, rest on pillars with capitals of ornamented foliage. The window labels also terminate in ornamental foliage. The row of Gothic arches beneath the clerestory have moulded surrounds with alternating decorations of foliage and king's heads. Along the clerestory

runs a band of decorative trefoil arches; at intervals small winged creatures protrude, gazing into the nave below. The protective pose of these strange little creatures, whose design origin dates back to the 14th century, gives the space-age viewer a fragile link with the beliefs and superstitions of the past.

During more than a century of history, a number of distinguished clergymen have served Fort Massey. Rev. Dr. Robert F. Burns who ministered for 17 years from 1875-1892 had an especially cheerful disposition; he also had an extremely portly physique which led to one mishap. Since it was not easy for him to climb up Tobin Street in winter, he asked a youth to haul him up the steep incline on a sled. Just as the summit was reached, the rope broke and the beloved minister coasted backwards to the bottom of the slope, luckily without injury. Following Rev. Dr. Burns was the Rev. Dr. Gandier who was, at 32 years of age, vigourously handsome and an eloquent speaker. The occasion of his first sermon on October 19, 1893, has been described as a memorable event: "Old and young were there; soldiers and sailors in uniform; students in droves and large representations from other churches. . . . The rich voice, the modest bearing, the perfect articulation, and spirit of reverence that possessed the minister combined to make a fitting atmosphere for the sermon . . ."

It was during Dr. Gandier's ministry in 1898, that the church hall was added to the back of the church at a cost of $19,144. This was felt to be a great improvement over the

basement quarters as "the smoke from the furnace did not have either the virtue or the fragrance of incense."

With the turn of the century, Rev. Dr. James W. Falconer came to Fort Massey. He was hailed as "the most erudite scholar and probably the choicest preacher in the long course of the river of years of the congregation." In 1907, he went on to Pine Hill Divinity Hall where he served as professor for 34 years. During those years he maintained his association with the church as Minister Emeritus. The Rev. Dr. Ross succeeded Dr. Falconer, and was minister during World War I and at the time of the Halifax Explosion in 1917. Several homeless women from the City's north end were housed in the basement of Fort Massey after the disaster. The church itself was damaged and extensive renovations were carried out. On November 10, 1918, a special service was held to celebrate the completion of the repairs.

From 1933 to 1940, the Rev. J. Norrie Anderson led the congregation. He was a native of Stornoway, Scotland, and had, for his active service in World War I, received the French Croix de Guerre "for remarkable courage." During the years of World War II, Rev. Gerald F. Rogers of New Glasgow, N.S., was minister. With the great influx of men and women of the Armed Forces into Halifax, Fort Massey, under Rev. Rogers, contributed its share to provide not only Sunday services but "through-the-week entertainment and hospitality." Pine Hill Divinity Hall conferred an honorary Doctor of Divinity degree on Rev. Rogers and on the Rev. Donald M. Sinclair who served Fort Massey for 21 years from 1948 to 1969.

While Rev. Sinclair presided, alterations were made to the interior of the church in the summer of 1951. Pews were re-arranged to provide a centre aisle; the choir stalls and the organ console were placed to create a chancel area at the front of the church. The original pulpit designed by David Stirling in 1873, was moved to the north side of the chancel and the lectern to the south side. Unused space in the basement was also transformed to accommodate the flourishing Sunday School. A great deal of the work was carried out by the men of the church.

No story of Fort Massey would be complete without mention of Mr. Harry Dean who served as organist for 46 years from 1906 to 1952. Mr. Dean had received honours at both the British School of Music and the Leipzig Conservatory, and while at Fort Massey, he was Director of the Halifax Conservatory of Music. Organ recitals were given, and on the church's 75th Anniversary, Mr. Dean directed the famous Hallelujah Chorus from Handel's Messiah. Fort Massey's prominence in the field of music is pleasantly ironic as, initially, there was considerable opposition to the introduction of a musical instrument into a service of worship. Finally, a pipe organ was installed in 1884. A new Casavant organ was procured in 1913 and rebuilt in 1951.

Fort Massey has an illustrious past in the history of its site and in its ministers and their congregations. The church structure itself is a fine example of the best traditions of Gothic architecture.

St. Joseph's, Glencoe Mills

It is amazing that, in the age of the space shuttle, there are still small communities in Nova Scotia where the only access is by a gravel road. In Cape Breton, one such gravel road, rather lengthy and punishing for a flimsy modern vehicle, is nevertheless well worth travelling. One reaches a scene of unequalled pastoral beauty. The undulating, green farmland is dotted with century-old farmhouses and enclosed by protecting forests. The church, which stands on the high point of land with its neat, fenced graveyard, is an architectural gem.

Early settlers came to the area during the 1820's, 1830's and 1840's. They originated from remote regions of Western Scotland including Lochaber and Moidart, and the islands of Eigg, Canna and Coll. Strangely though, the first name for the settled area was "Turk Settlement" which, understandably, was not popular with the inhabitants. Pioneer Archibald MacDonald, who had arrived from Badenoch, Scotland in 1820, undertook to have the name changed. On April 18, 1872, it was recorded in the Statutes of Nova Scotia that: "Turk Settlement in the county of Inverness shall hereafter be called and known by the name of Glencoe." Archibald MacDonald had chosen the name in honour of his father's birthplace in the homeland.

The Highlanders who came to the Glencoe area were primarily Roman Catholics. They had come to the new land seeking freedom from the religious turmoil and cruelty of the powerful lairds. In the early days, Glencoe was a mission of the neighbouring, larger communities of Mabou and Port Hood. From 1896 up to the present day, Glencoe has been a mission of Brook Village, where the priest resides.

St. Joseph's Church was probably built shortly after October 14, 1873, the date when the deed for the land was signed by Hugh and Angus MacDonald. Two acres of land, including a portion owned by Hugh MacDonald, were sold by Angus MacDonald for the sum of $40.

The lumber was readily available from the forest which was close at hand, and each parishioner contributed to the labour of constructing the church. Boards were hand-planed, and up and down saws used. Alex MacKinnon of Broad Cove worked as a carpenter as did Malcolm MacDonald.

The carpenters must have been well trained as the church shows a level of sophistication and detail beyond many of the rural churches. The side and front elevations are graced with long, mullioned Gothic windows accented with bold label mouldings. The main entrance is also a Gothic arch with a label moulding, and decorative quatre-foil motifs in the small window over the door.

The steeple is truly unique in Nova Scotia. The tower, which is very narrow in depth, is expertly ornamented with a long, triple-arched, Gothic window and a small double-arched Gothic window above. Extending high above the roof-line is the picturesque bell-cote with an open Gothic arch and steeply-pitched roof.

The reason for the use of such a steeple design is not easy to trace directly. Certainly the Anglicans used bell-cotes fairly frequently on their rural churches of the mid-19th century. But the Anglican style of bell-cote was much smaller and always perched saddle-back on the roof. In contrast, the dramatic use of the bell-cote extending upward from a tower, as on St. Joseph's, is more akin to the French "clocher à peine" style. The French style usually had two or more belfry openings, thus giving it the name "belfry like a comb." Perhaps the carpenters who designed St. Joseph's had seen pictures of such belfries, or perhaps it is an imaginative creation which is reminiscent of the French style by accident.

Whatever the exact roots for the stylistic elements, the clever use of a variety of Gothic arches, single, double and triple, along with the high bell-cote, all combine to make St. Joseph's a magnificent composition.

Inside, slender pillars support the ceiling which forms a high rounded arch above the central aisle. The ceiling was constructed by Alex MacDonnell and John Beaton of Judique. A single gallery runs across the back of the nave; the gallery front is decorated with a row of moulded Gothic arches. The pews are straight-backed but have nicely sculptured arms; the sides have a raised Gothic arch pattern. The walls are not plastered but the wide planks are painted in warm tones of gold and cream which add a finished appearance to an authentic country feature.

St. Joseph's is well maintained; its original and unique architectural features have been carefully conserved. Many of the parishioners, direct descendants of the pioneer settlers, still farm the land like their ancestors before them. With the exception of modern automobiles which may occasionally traverse the old gravel roads, the 20th century has not greatly intruded on the old-fashioned peace and beauty of the Glencoe area.

Westminster,
New Glasgow

The Victorian Gothic elegance of Westminster Church in New Glasgow does not indicate outwardly the early pioneer beginnings of its Presbyterian congregation. Similarily, the quiet residential setting of the church, in close proximity to Trinity United and St. Andrew's (Kirk) Church, belies the difficult, often disruptive, evolution of Presbyterianism in the community.

Westminster's roots go back to the log church built by Rev. Dr. James McGregor, in 1787, on the Stellarton Road just west of New Glasgow. Dr. McGregor, who had come out from Scotland in response to a petition from the settlers, was the first Presbyterian minister to establish a congregation in Pictou County. Dr. McGregor belonged to the Antiburgher sept of Presbyterianism; from 1747 to 1820, Antiburghers in Scotland did not agree that all Christians be required to take an oath of loyalty to the established Church of Scotland. Bur Dr. MacGregor ministered to both types of Presbyterians in Pictou County until the arrival, in 1817, of Rev. Donald Allan Fraser, the first Church of Scotland minister.

In 1803, Dr. James McGregor's congregation moved to a frame church which was later named James Church in honour of its founder. This church, situated at Irishtown (later Plymouth), served until a new James Church was built on MacLean Street, New Glasgow, in 1852. But, several years before the new James Church was constructed, the "storm of schism" had already burst in the congregation. The exact cause of the controversy is now obscure, but various possible reasons, all having to do with the Rev. David Roy, still remain.

Rev. Roy had taken over after the death of Dr. McGregor. The fire of contention may have been fuelled because Rev. Roy could not speak Gaelic and was a poor disciplinarian in Session Meetings, or because he was a bachelor and ignored the charms of the unmarried daughters in the congregation. At any rate, two elders of the church, James McGregor, son of Dr. McGregor, and Hugh MacKay appeared before the Pictou Presbytery and alleged that they had not gone to church for some time (one year in the case of McGregor and three months in the case of MacKay) due to the Rev. David Roy. There was no solution to the rift, and Rev. Roy recorded briefly, without anger, that "James McGregor and Hugh MacKay with a number of families were disjointed from the congregation in the spring of 1845."

The breakaway group, 26 people in all, formed Primitive Church, and a structure by that name was built at the corner of Provost and Forbes streets in 1849. On the morning of April 19, 1874, New Glasgow suffered a disastrous fire which levelled a large section of the town including Primitive Church. After the fire, the congregation of Primitive Church joined with the congregation of John Knox Church which, itself, had been formed as a result of a split in St. Andrew's Church of Scotland congregation in 1845.

The congregations of Primitive and John Knox churches became known as the

United Presbyterian Church and, as such, constructed a new building on Temperance Street. The magnificent Gothic structure, known as the United Church, and later Westminster Church, was opened for service on January 9, 1876.

The builders of Westminster Church were Hugh Ross and Captain George McKenzie. At the time, Hugh Ross was a member of the Session or governing body of the church, while Capt. George McKenzie was a member of the congregation and a master shipwright. Indeed, McKenzie was a colourful and prominent figure during the grand era of New Glasgow's history, from 1830 to 1875, when shipbuilding was the chief industry.

George McKenzie, whose father John McKenzie had been one of the founders of New Glasgow, first came to prominence at the age of nineteen. When a vessel got stuck while being launched, the youthful McKenzie volunteered to solve the problem after all others had given up in despair having exhausted both their ingenuity and their mechanical equipment. George McKenzie succeeded in launching the vessel at the very next tide and earned an enviable reputation. He sailed for some years as Captain on vessels bound for both the West Indies and Britain and finally settled down to building sailing ships at the shipyards owned by his brother-in-law James Carmichael. McKenzie built some of the biggest vessels of the time, including the 1,400 ton Hamilton Campbell Kidston and the Magna Charta.

Westminster Church was the child of Capt. George McKenzie's last retirement years and a culmination of his impressive building talents. McKenzie himself is said to have once remarked about the church. " 'Tis a ship but we built it upside down." The truth of this statement is particularly obvious in the interior.

The arrangement of the roof trusses and arched supporting braces bear a marked resemblance to the framing members of a large, flat-bottomed vessel with a curved hull. The massive, arched roof braces were hand-carved in Merigomish and lugged by double teams of horses a distance of 20 kilometres to New Glasgow.

Other interesting features of the interior include the round Peace window with its central, stained-glass motif of a dove with an olive branch. The two large stained-glass windows on either side of the nave were added in 1921 to commemorate the war dead of World War I and the Hon. James D. McGregor a grandson of Rev. Dr. James McGregor, who became a prominent Liberal politician, Senator, and Lieutenant Governor of Nova Scotia. The three ornate mahogany pulpit chairs were rescued from the fire before Primitive Church was destroyed. A superb Casavant organ, installed in 1909 and remodelled in 1926, has 96 speaking pipes on each of its 36 ranks. Because of the organ, Westminster Church was occasionally rented for concerts; stars from the Metropolitan Opera, like Richard Crooks and Madam Galligurchi, sang in the church, and Ronald Murdock from Merigomish, who became an internationally-known tenor, launched his career there.

The light oak pews, which form concentric semi-circles about the pulpit and dias, were rearranged to face the west side of the church from 1909 to 1917. This change was made to accommodate the preacher who had a weak voice and wanted to be closer to his flock. After his term was over, the pews were restored to their original position; at the same time, the pulpit area was slightly enlarged and a new, sloped floor was laid over the old in order to raise the back of the church by 26 inches to increase visibility.

The exterior of Westminster Church has a wealth of Gothic embellishment. Yet the lavish detailing, neither heavy nor gaudy, creates an overall sense of lightness and good taste, akin to precisely-crafted embroidery. The front façade is particularly attractive with its decorated double entrance which is flanked by slim Gothic label windows and topped by the large, rose window centred above. The corner buttresses end in peaked finials which extend well above the roofline.

The side steeple, which appears to be almost freestanding, is very imposing. It rises 109 feet and is richly ornamented. There are long, mullioned Gothic windows incorporating the same six-petal flower design that one finds on the two main entrance doors. The corner buttresses of the square tower finish in peaked finials which lead the eye up to the octagonal belfry. The slim belfry openings are accented by Gothic peaks above, which again lead the viewer's eye upwards to the spire.

Curiously, the main body of the church was connected to a house which existed on a lot prior to the construction of the church. The house now fulfills the function of a church hall and its rooms are used for Sunday School and social purposes. A gymnasium was added to the hall in 1900.

In 1925, not one of the three Presbyterian churches in New Glasgow voted to join the United Church of Canada, though some members from each church broke away to form Trinity United Church. At Westminster, it was a lengthy and bitter struggle which resulted in a fist fight in front of the pulpit between the minister and a visiting minister from Summerside, P.E.I., who had come to conduct the voting. Of all the Presbyterian congregations in Nova Scotia, the Westminster congregation, in a vote of 263 to 73, provided the largest majority against union.

After the debacle, it became necessary that the church, then called "United," must change its name. The decision was not easy; voting on a new name from a choice of five possible names took seven weeks. The name "Westminster" was finally chosen and is entirely appropriate, as it recalls the Westminster Assembly in 1645 which had laid down the doctrines of the Presbyterian faith.

Westminster Church is a staunch stronghold of Presbyterianism, clad in the delicate details of Gothic artistry. While the great sailing ships that Capt. George McKenzie built have all gone, the church he built remains, and has been recognized as "the finest piece of Gothic architecture in wood in Eastern Canada."

Gibbons' Churches,
Baddeck,
Jordan Falls,
Diligent River,
Moose River

ANGLICAN
CHURCH

The story of the Reverend Simon Gibbons and the five distinctive churches that were built during the twenty-year period of his ministry has given Nova Scotia an interesting and distinctive legacy.

Simon Gibbons' life itself had a dramatic and legendary quality. Born in 1853, in Red Bay, Labrador, Gibbons was the son of an English sailor and an Eskimo woman. His extraordinary intelligence as a small boy attracted the attention of the Anglican Bishop Field of Newfoundland who undertook to give Gibbons a higher education. He attended Cambridge University in England, where his brilliant scholarship led him to attain a professorship at McGill University in Montreal.

But Gibbons must have known, perhaps through Bishop Field, of the critical need for missionary work in the rugged, sparsely-populated areas of Cape Breton, for he soon decided to devote his life to the church rather than to the classroom. He established a mission which extended from Baddeck 120 kilometres up the rocky and mountainous coast to Cape North.

Travelling in this remote area in the 19th century was particularly difficult; Rev. Simon Gibbons often journeyed on foot or on snowshoes, scaling the steep headland of Cape Smokey between Baddeck and Neil's Harbour, where he usually spent three weeks alternately. He always stopped en route to visit a lighthouse keeper and his wife near Ingonish. One stormy winter night, two weeks before the "parson" was due, the lighthouse keeper sensed trouble. Even though his wife protested that there should be no cause for alarm, the lighthouse keeper and his dog set out to search Smokey. Near the summit, they found and followed snowshoe tracks which led to the edge of a thirty-foot precipice. At the foot of the precipice, Rev. Gibbons lay unconscious in the snow. He was quickly transported to the lighthouse keeper's abode where he was nursed back to health.

Gibbons began his mission in Victoria County in 1877, and the Anglican church at Baddeck was constructed under his direction. St. Peter-St. John, as it is now called, is not a large church, and its small scale is enhanced by its pleasing, country Gothic style. Slim Gothic windows and ornamental buttresses decorate the exterior walls and the bell-tower. The cladding is vertical-lined board and batten which is not common in Nova Scotia. But even more uncommon is the Rhenish helm roof, a four-sided, gabled roof which appears to be formed by uniting four large, diamond-shaped sections together.

The architectural roots for the Rhenish helm roof are noteworthy. In Britain there is only one existing example of a Rhenish helm roof; at Sompting in Sussex, an ancient Saxon church which dates back to the 11th century has such a roof on its bell-tower. This roof style is said to be the original type of finish used on church towers of the Saxon period. The term "Rhenish helm roof" is used because of the similarity of the style to many examples in the Rhineland.

Rev. Simon Gibbons may have seen or known about the Saxon church at Sompting, as he had spent some time studying and lecturing in England. In fact, Gibbons had returned from one lecture tour with a carved, Saxon baptismal font for his Baddeck church. The font, still in the church, is said to be 700 years old.

A second explanation for Gibbons' penchant for the unusual roof style may be even more plausible. From 1771, Moravian missionaries from Germany were well established on the northern coast of Labrador. As a bright Inuit boy growing up on the coast of Labrador, Gibbons would likely have seen pictures of German churches in the homeland with the particular bell-towers and Rhenish helm roofs. The style continued to persist into the present century. At Nain, Labrador, in 1923, a Moravian church was built with a square bell-tower and the stylistic Rhenish roof.

During his pastorate in Cape Breton, Gibbons lectured in such far flung places as England, France, and New York in order to raise funds for the support of his mission. He must have created a good deal of interest wherever he went as his physical appearance was striking and his methods were innovative. He was of a short build with a round face, black hair and a large moustache. On one occasion when he had been invited to give a service in another parish, he arrived to find his letter of acceptance had not been delivered and no service was planned. Undaunted, he borrowed a fur coat and headed for the church. The sight of a short Eskimo man in an oversized fur coat walking through the town on a hot summer's day quickly drew a crowd of followers. By the time he donned his clerical vestments, a congregation awaited him. On another occasion, while in England, he had an audience with Queen Victoria. He wore a heavy fur coat, cap, and mittens to show her Majesty what the people of Cape Breton wore in winter.

About 1884, Rev. Gibbons was appointed rector at Jordan Falls, Shelburne County, on Nova Scotia's South Shore. He found the old church there in a state of disrepair. It was moved off the site by 12 yoke of oxen and work was begun on the new Holy Trinity Church. Built by William Cox, George Collupy, Charles Hardy, and Amos Pentz, probably all local men of the parish, Holy Trinity is a work of art. Like Gibbons' church in Baddeck, it is small-scale, with narrow Gothic windows and a side entrance and tower. But that relatively plain, unembellished design was adapted by its builders to include the rector's wish for a Rhenish helm bell-tower roof as well as the highly decorative details so typical of Shelburne County.

The bell-tower has three distinct sections, which become more ornamental as the eye travels upwards. The lowest section containing the entrance porch has the Gothic arches of the doorway and side windows, as well as some pilaster detail and a partial bellcast-flared top which is connected to the central section. There, one sees pilaster detail,

diagonal clapboard, and a truncated gabled top. This section is surmounted by the 'pièce de résistance,' the octagonal belfry with Gothic openings and a stunning double Rhenish helm roof, lavishly decorated with cornice work and diamond shingle patterns.

Holy Trinity Church was consecrated in 1889 by Bishop Frederick Courtney, the fifth bishop of Nova Scotia. But by that time, the Rev. Gibbons had already been transferred to the Parrsboro parish on the Fundy Shore. Like his former Cape Breton parish, the Parrsboro parish was enormous, spanning Cumberland and Colchester counties and stretching some 120 kilometres from Apple River and Advocate to Onslow near Truro.

During Gibbons' term as rector of the Parrsboro parish, from 1888 to 1896, two churches were built on the Fundy shore with the characteristic Rhenish helm bell-tower roof. At Diligent River, a small settlement about 7 miles west of Parrsboro, St. John's Anglican Church was built in 1890. St. John's is the plainest of the Gibbons' churches, lacking, for example, the chancel extension which the others have. Recently, too, the original clapboard has been covered with modern siding and all vestiges of the corner pilasters and brackets removed. Yet, the church still stands with its distinctive bell-tower, and those missing authentic features could be restored.

At Moose River, about 10 miles east of Parrsboro, the diminutive St. Mark's Anglican was built in 1894. At the time of its

construction, there were about 12 families in the little lumbering centre. Land for the church was given by Benjamin Roberts, William Roberts, and John W. Smith. The men of the community built the church with their own hands, the married men donating 25 days of labour and the single men giving 15 days. James Roberts and Benjamin Roberts completed the interior. Set well back from the road on spacious grounds, the small, white St. Mark's Church, with its freshly painted clapboard walls, its narrow Gothic door, slim Gothic windows, and special bell-tower, is a very picturesque scene.

A fifth church, St. Thomas Anglican at Mooseland, in Halifax County, was built in 1887 with a Gibbons' bell-tower. But Gibbons had no known connection with this church. It was constructed during the ministry of Dr. Edward Ball. However, the very fact that St. Thomas was built exactly at the time when Gibbons was preaching and building his own churches suggests that Gibbons must have influenced its design. More than likely Dr. Ball, a contemporary and fellow clergyman of Gibbons, knew and admired him. Perhaps, too, he admired his taste for interesting architectural features and decided to duplicate them. Or perhaps Gibbons himself, who gave numerous guest appearances, suggested the design of the bell-tower to Dr. Ball.

Rev. Simon Gibbons' death was untimely and resulted from a dramatic incident. In 1896, at 43 years of age, Gibbons died from injuries he received when stopping the runaway horse and carriage of two maiden ladies.

Rev. Simon Gibbons was the first Inuit to become an Anglican preacher. He was a gentleman and a scholar. He was a charismatic spiritual leader with a definite preference for the unusual Rhenish helm roof style. The churches in Nova Scotia with Gibbons' bell-towers are a fitting tribute to an extraordinary pioneer clergyman.

Photos:

St. Peter-St. John, Baddeck, page 114
Holy Trinity, Jordan Falls, page 117
St. Mark's, Moose River, page 118
St. John's, Diligent River, page 120 (right)
St. Thomas, Mooseland, page 120 (left)

St. James',
Great Village

One difference between an architect-designed church and one designed by a local builder, it that an architect does not mix styles. For instance, Gothic arches would not be used with classical pilasters. This is not to say that the majority of churches, which are built in the vernacular tradition where styles are often combined, are any less attractive. But it does explain why the embellishments of St. James' are purely from the Gothic style.

Regardless of whether or not a building is architect-designed, the calibre of workmanship is an important factor as well. In the case of St. James', one has only to look at the moulded detailing over the front door to recognize that skilled carpenters were employed. Many of the workers were, in fact, ship carpenters and shipwrights. Great Village was well known in distant seaports for its sailing ships and sea captains; when money was needed to built St. James', generous donations were received from foreign shipping companies.

The church did not actually receive its name until 1925, when the Presbyterian congregation joined the United Church of Canada. The name St. James' was chosen in honour of the Rev. James MacLean who was minister between 1875 and 1900. It was through his inspiration and encouragement that the church was built.

St. James' United stands as the architectural focus of a charming village. A visitor leaves Great Village reluctantly, memorizing its images and promising to return.

St. James',
Mahone Bay

PEACE BE WITHIN THY WALLS
HOLINESS TO THE LORD

Mahone Bay, located along the South Shore of the province, is one of the loveliest coastal areas in Nova Scotia. It is an area comprised of hundreds of islands and intriguing coves. The town of Mahone Bay, on the western side of the bay, may be approached by water through a long harbour or by the main road which runs along the water's edge. Situated in the most prominent position in the town at the very head of the harbour is St. James' Anglican church.

The original inhabitants of the town of Mahone Bay were Indians who had one encampment near the present town and a second at Indian Point. In addition, there was a small French settlement near Mader's Cove. But it was not until 1754 that the present town was actually established. Twenty prominent residents came to Mahone Bay in vessels under the command of Ephriam Cook, from the state of New York.

In the days of early settlement, church services were held locally in private homes and in a schoolhouse, by the clergy from Lunenburg. Often, the faithful would make the journey to Lunenburg to attend services at St. John's Church; they would walk the distance barefooted in order not to ruin their footwear. Only at the outskirts of town would they put on their stockings and shoes.

In 1883, the Anglicans built their first church in Mahone Bay, a small frame building which they named St. James'. This building served the congregation until 1887, when a site for a new church was chosen and the present St. James' was constructed.

Rev. W.H. Snyder was the rector at the time the new St. James' was constructed, and Rev. E.A. Harris was curate. It was Rev. Harris' brother, William Critchlow Harris, who was appointed architect for the new church.

William Harris was born in 1854 at Hemer Terrace, Bootle, near Liverpool in England. His family moved to Canada and settled in Prince Edward Island when he was two years old. One brother, Robert, later became a celebrated portrait painter in the Canada of his day. William became an important 19th and early 20th century Canadian architect whose specialty was the design of churches.

William Harris' initiation into the field of architecture began in 1870 at the age of 16 years when he went to Halifax as an indentured apprentice in the office of well-known architect David Stirling. In 1877, Stirling and Harris formed a partnership which Harris left after five years.

Harris lived his whole life in Prince Edward Island and Halifax, except for two years when he worked in Winnipeg. He was a Victorian architect who developed a personal style of design, blending elements from a variety of sources. Although Harris became a noted ecclesiastical architect, his work also included private homes and commercial buildings. During his career, he designed and built 116 buildings, 17 of which were churches built in Nova Scotia. A total of 90 of his buildings are still standing today.

In the new St. James' Church in Mahone Bay, Harris set a high standard of construction when he specified, "the foundation walls and piers (were) to be built of the best rubble masonry of good native stone, laid, bedded, and flushed up in good lime mortar and pointed on both sides." Harris also stated that "the whole of the timber and lumber (were) to be of the best description, free from sap, shakes, large, loose, or dead knots, thoroughly seasoned."

The church measured 42 feet wide and 100 feet long with a tower standing 91 feet high. The estimated cost of the church at the time of construction was $8,000. As an indication of the enthusiasm for the new building, all but $1,000 was raised prior to construction.

The striking impression of the interior of St. James' is its surprising spaciousness, resulting from the broad, clear span of the roof and the large windows. Major framing members are spruce, and the roof trusses are completed with hammer-beams. A variety of hardwoods make up the interior finish, and according to the original specification, included birch, maple, ash, and beech. Pine was used for the pews and spruce for the ceiling finish and sanctuary walls.

Harris was very conscious of acoustics in designing church buildings. In the sanctuary at St. James', he fixed the wall panelling to a hardwood backup wall. His theory was that this would amplify the sound of the speaker much the same way as the sound of a reverberating violin string is amplified within the box of the violin.

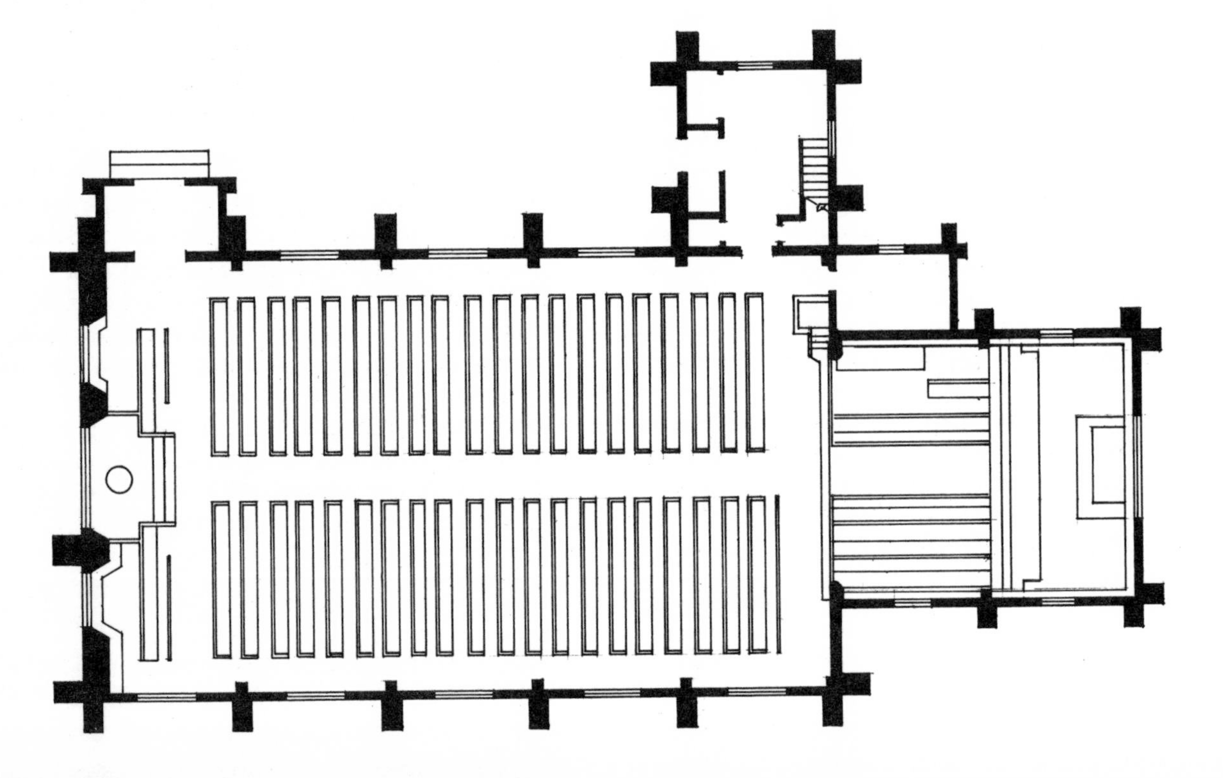

Interior colours are as they were originally. The woodwork has a natural finish; the chancel arch mouldings and trim at the east window are painted blue, and the walls are a soft green. The exterior was originally painted grey but is now beige with brown and red accents. The bands of different colours on the spire are a typical characteristic of Harris' churches.

From the exterior, the design of the church is embellished by a regular series of broad arched windows, alternating with buttresses. The exterior cladding is board and batten. The spire is of the early English "broach" type. The steeple is situated at the shoulder of the chancel, which, because of the orientation of the building, dominates the entrance to the town both by road and water. Harris' biographer, Robert C. Tuck, noted both that the steeple of St. James' is "one of William Harris' loveliest creations" and that "the church as a whole is the crowning achievement of the early period of his career."

St. James' is one of a trio of churches at the head of Mahone Bay. The two other churches are St. John's Lutheran and Trinity United. Together these churches form one of the most photographed scenic views in the province.

Mahone Bay is rich in history and tradition. The pride of its residents is evident in the architecture of their buildings and most of all in the beauty of their places of worship.

Peniel United,
Five Islands

The village of Five Islands in Colchester County is in the heart of one of the most scenic and ecologically interesting areas of Nova Scotia. Situated on the shores of the Minas Basin, the village overlooks a string of five, beautiful islands, which, according to legend, were formed when Glooscap, the giant Micmac demigod, flung handfuls of earth into the sea. On these islands and along the rocky coast, the amateur rockhound may readily find treasures like smooth red jasper, blue lace agates, and sparkling amethyst crystals. It is in this area, too, that visitors may see the highest tides in the world, with the salt water rising over fifty feet at one time.

It seems perfectly appropiate that amid such natural grandeur, the village of Five Islands should have a magnificent man-made church with a very high, graceful spire. Peniel United Church was built in 1890 and is the third church on the site.

In 1782, William Corbett, A Scottish Presbyterian, had been the first settler to come to Five Islands. In time, other Scottish and Northern Irish settlers followed. The first settled minister, Rev. Andrew Kerr, came out from Scotland in 1817, the year that the first Presbyterian church was built. It was a large, square meeting house that was only "partly finished inside" and had box pews. This church was used until 1848 when steps were taken to build a second church. When completed a few years later, it was said to have been a two-storey building which "looked like a factory" outside but was "well finished inside."

By 1888, the congregation wanted an even larger and better church. Extra land was purchased for $65.00, and four men, Daniel Hill, A.F. Bentley, W. McLellan, and John Graham, were appointed to supervise the construction. The builder of the church was B.T. Creelman of Portaupique, a village just a few miles along the coast.

On Wednesday, July 9, 1890, the third church was formally opened, after it had been completely finished and furnished at a total cost of $5,400. A special name, Peniel, was chosen for the new place of worship. Taken from the thirty-second book of Genesis, Peniel was the place where Jacob saw God face to face and was saved.

Peniel United Church is truly a product of its area. The large structure with its soaring spire gives the immediate impression that it was built sturdily with quantities of good lumber having been used unsparingly. This is probably quite accurate as lumbering was a major industry in the area. When lumbering was at its best, it would not have been unusual to see "fifty deal teams on the road at one time, hauling lumber from the mills to the wharves to be loaded on ships for export trade."

The second impression that Peniel United imparts to the viewer is that its tasteful ornamentation has been carefully crafted by experts. This is undoubtedly true too, for there were a number of highly-skilled ships' carpenters in Five Islands because of the shipbuilding industry. Between 1841 and 1910, 26 locally-made ships — brigentines, schooners, barques, and sloops — were launched. The largest was the barque "Mevado" which weighed 674 tons and was launched in 1871 at the peak of the shipbuilding era.

A third aspect of the church, which though less important is nevertheless obvious, is the smooth well-painted look about it. That, too, is probably traditional. The oldest paint-manufacturing firm in Canada, Henderson and Potts, known later as Brandram-Henderson, was originally located at Lower Five Islands. There it was near the shipbuilding industry and close to the barytes mine on the banks of the nearby Bass River. Sulphate of barytes was made into a pigment which was in turn mixed with white lead in the paint-making process.

Architecturally, Peniel United is classical in plan with a central tower and windows placed symmetrically on either side. The exterior is richly embellished with both classical and Gothic details. For example, the front gable end is pedimented in the classical mode, while the windows on the second storey are Gothic in style with label mouldings. The corner pilasters on the main body of the church, as well as on the bell tower, display an interesting blend of the two styles with classical capitals and decorative pointed Gothic mouldings at intervals along the length of each pilaster. A very attractive and unusual feature is the stringcourse moulding which runs in horizontal bands around the body of the church linking the Gothic pilaster ornaments at each side and accentuating the window tops.

The steeple has a long, mullioned Gothic window with a large, circular decoration above and an open belfry with Gothic arches. The landmark spire rises to a height of 120 feet. It is decorated with slim, Gothic arches and may be described as a "broach spire," with an elongated roof.

In comparison to the exterior, the interior is very plain, almost Spartan in appearance. On entering the vestibule, two flights of stairs, to the right and left, lead up to the main sanctuary; a third staircase, straight ahead, leads downward to a spacious basement, Sunday School, and social area. In the sanctuary, the blond, semi-circular pews are made of ash and could seat about 320 persons. In a departure from custom, the pews face the two entrance doors; the platform containing the pulpit and the choir loft above are located between the entrance doors along what is normally the "back" wall of the church. The lack of interior embellishment gives a feeling of open countryside like the field beside the church, and it is totally in keeping with the strict Presbyterian ethic.

In 1925, the Peniel Church joined the United Church of Canada. In 1964, renovations were made to the basement; a modern kitchen and lavatory were installed, and the entire area was painted and panelled. Several men of the congregation donated many weekend hours to work on the project. Over the years, the Sewing Circle or Ladies Aid have contributed many thousands of dollars for the upkeep of the church through fund raising activities. With the increasing importance of the blueberry and maple syrup industries of the area, one can imagine that the ladies of Peniel United would provide the most delicious pie socials and pancake breakfasts!

Undoubtedly, Peniel United will continue to be well cared for, and its high, slender spire will continue to dominate the horizon at Five Islands.

St. Ambrose Cathedral, Yarmouth

The town of Yarmouth was first settled in 1761 by Americans of the Congregationalist and Baptist denominations. By the early 1800's, a number of Irish Catholic families had made Yarmouth their home. Among the Irish, with names like Sullivan, Callaghan and Halloran, there were Dominic Devitt, a tailor, and Edmund Lonergan, a merchant; it was in the homes of these two men that Roman Catholic worship services were first held. From 1797 to 1839, Abbé Jean-Mandé Sigogne, the indefatigable missionary from the French Shore, provided spiritual guidance.

In 1845, Mr. Lonergan purchased the carpenter's workshop of Benjamin Bingay and then transferred the ownership to Father John Carmody, the first resident priest. For the sum of £100, Father Carmody had the workshop remodelled to serve as a church. When the converted workshop became inadequate for the size of the congregation, a wooden church was built on the site in 1862. This church was Gothic in style and known as All Saints' until its name was changed to St. Ambrose by Father Edward J. McCarthy who became pastor in 1883. By 1889, this modest church was too small for the burgeoning parish, and Father McCarthy undertook the building of a second St. Ambrose which is the present structure.

A new and spacious site was chosen at the corner of Albert and Green streets. The cornerstone was laid by Archbishop Cornelius O'Brien on July 8, 1889. Construction must have progressed quickly, for only a few months later, the first service was held at midnight on Christmas Eve of 1889. At that time the congregation met in the basement as work on the main sanctuary was continuing. Architect for the project was J.C. Dumaresq of Halifax. James E. Huestis of Yarmouth directed the construction. Benjamin Ritchie, also of Yarmouth was responsible for the ornamentation. The estimated cost of the project was about $20,000.

J.C. Dumaresq was not only a prolific architect who had designed buildings in both Nova Scotia and New Brunswick, but he was capable of great diversity of style. Compare, for example, the wooden, Gothic style of St. James', built in 1883 for the Presbyterian congregation at Great Village, with the purely Romanesque brick structure of St. Ambrose. Though the seating capacity for St. Ambrose was average, the original design incorporated many grand elements. On either side of the front elevation rose two round turrets with domed roofs, the left turret rising higher than the right. Although both turrets, which contain staircases, have since been shortened, and are now of equal height, the classical front façade is still attractive.

The central gable is pedimented with moulded dentil trim and a rondel window. Below the pediment, three classical windows grace the façade; the centre window is large and decorated with a keystone arch fashioned in light sandstone, while two narrow windows with simpler sandstone arches complete the trio on either side. Below the windows, three

doors of matching classical style continue the theme. The central door has a sandstone pediment above while the two narrower adjacent doors have plain sandstone arches. Corner pilasters add a final classical touch to the edifice.

The original plans called for a transept on each side elevation. The design of the transepts was in harmony with the front elevation and included three long round-headed windows, corner pilasters and a decorative pedimented gable. When the church needed more space in 1908, the back section of the church was moved backwards and two additional transepts were constructed, adding an extra 75 feet in length. The extension, which took two years to complete, was done tastefully with the style of the new transepts exactly matching the old. The total cost of the enlargement amounted to $8,181, almost half the original cost of construction. In 1910, Edward McCarthy who had become Archbishop of Halifax, returned to the church that he had built, to dedicate the new extension.

Over the years, the interior has received changes too, but not so many as to spoil the intrinsic beauty of the design. The old pews were replaced with more comfortable light oak ones to match the new oak wainscotting. Stained glass windows were added, depicting a number of the Saints, including St. Ambrose. St. Ambrose was a fourth century Bishop of Milan who had great compassion for the down-trodden but was intolerant of the abuse of public office. Also in possession of the church is a magnificent crucifix which was carved in 1890 by James Doane, a widely recognized Yarmouth artist.

The most striking feature of the interior is the vaulted ceiling with rounded Romanesque arches. The colonnades of supporting pillars on each side of the nave lead the eye forward to the canopied ceiling behind the altar. The square pillars themselves are particularly fine, with decorative reeding and ornate Corinthian capitals. Pilaster detailing along the walls reinforces the visual effect of the pillars. The ceiling vaults are also highlighted by painted borders and "fleur de lis" motifs in shades of green, gold and cream.

In 1953, the new diocese of Yarmouth was created and St. Ambrose was chosen as its cathedral. From its humble beginnings in a converted carpenter's workshop, the parish had achieved a high goal. And the parish church was more than suitable for its role as cathedral.

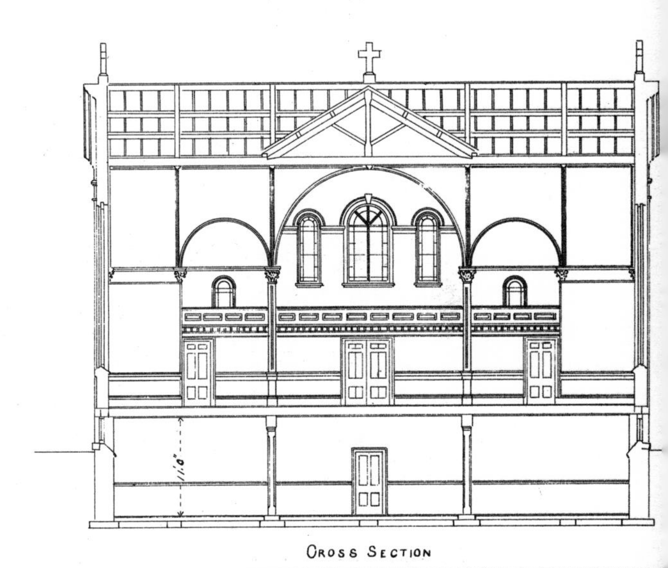

CROSS SECTION

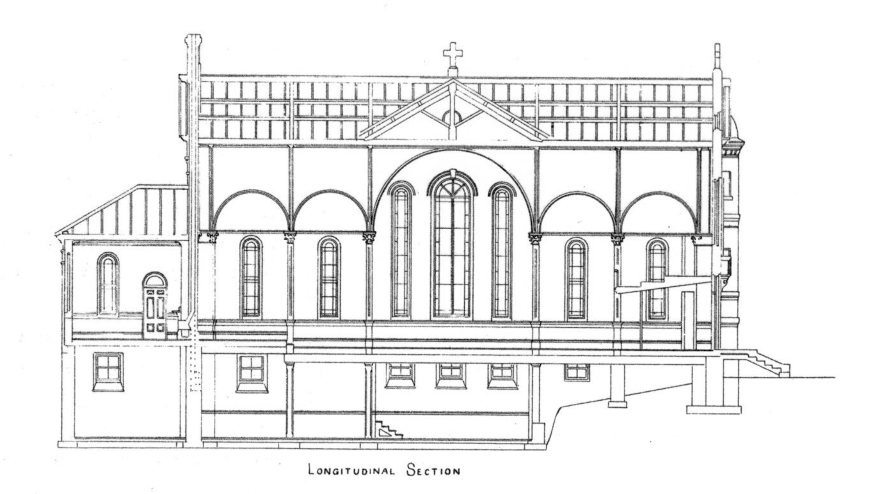
Longitudinal Section

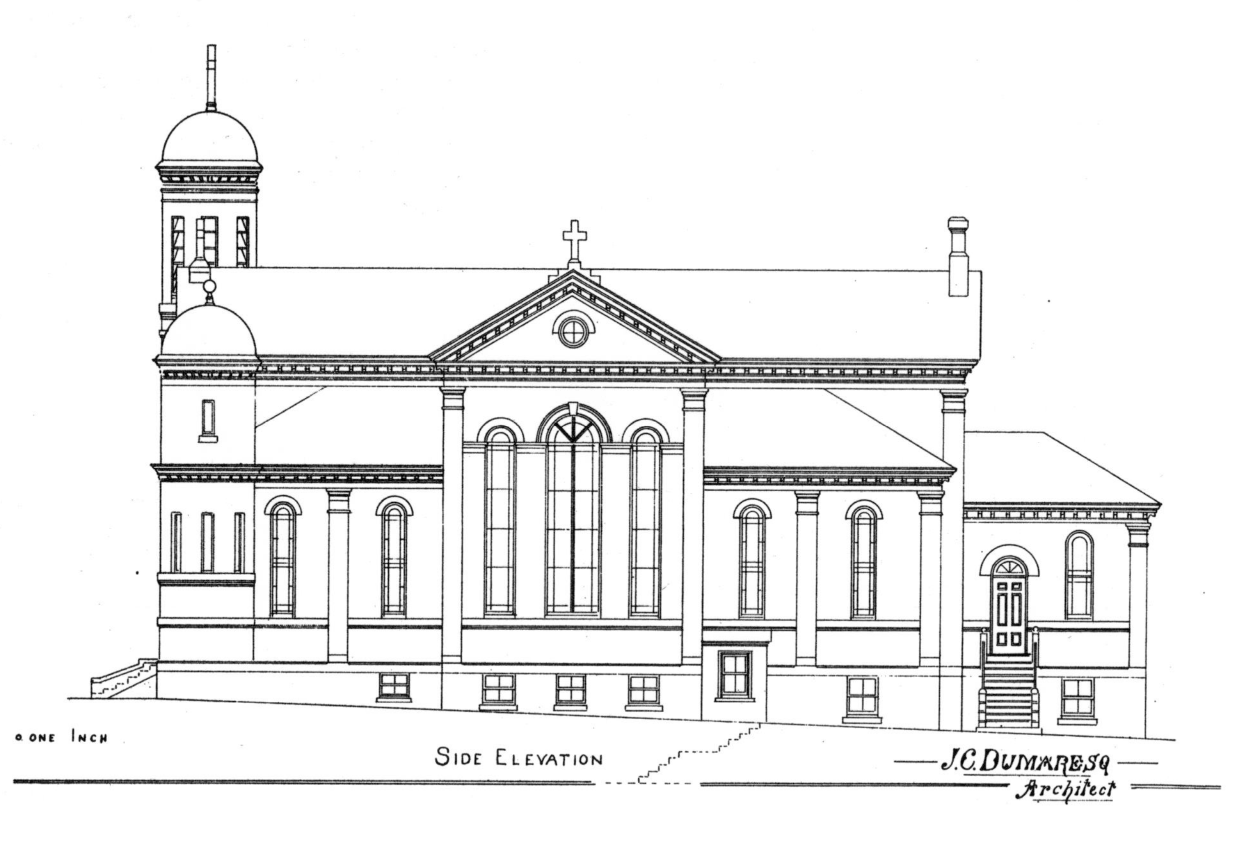
0 One Inch
Side Elevation
J.C. Dumaresq
Architect

Eglise St. Pierre, Cheticamp

The Acadian community of Chéticamp is magnificently situated, with a harbour sheltered by Chéticamp Island, and a backdrop of the Cape Breton highlands. Just beyond Chéticamp, the Cabot Trail, the province's most dramatic scenic route, begins. It was to this incredibly beautiful part of the northern coast that Acadian settlers came to found Chéticamp in 1782.

The first place of worship, built by the early settlers in 1790, was a small log chapel, and the first Roman Catholic missionary was Jean-Baptiste Allain who arrived from France in 1797. By 1810, the log chapel was replaced by a frame church, named St. Apollinaire, which was constructed about two miles from the present village. In 1861, a third church, made of stone, was built on the present site, an elevated plateau in the centre of the community. This church was reported to have been about 100 feet in length and "purely gothic" in style. The fourth, and present St. Peter's Church (Eglise St. Pierre), was erected in 1893, during the 34-year tenure of Father Pierre Fiset.

Born in Lorette, France, in 1840, Father Fiset was ordained at Antigonish in 1864, and appointed parish priest of Chéticamp in 1875. When Father Fiset arrived in Chéticamp, he found the hard-working inhabitants burdened with poverty. While trying to make a living through fishing and farming, they were unable to overcome the debts owed on needed machinery and equipment, and the prices they received for the fish and farm produce were poor.

The energetic Father Fiset immediately undertook the task of solving the economic ills of the community. He taught self-sufficiency and encouraged the fishermen to build their own boats; he had a grist mill built so that the wheat could be ground locally, and he started gypsum quarrying on a commercial scale. He also taught co-operative farming and marketing to increase the output and gain better prices. He operated a model farm on Chéticamp Island where he used scientific methods and good management principles. And he was not afraid to dirty his own hands as well. Wearing old boots and work clothes, he often hauled seaweed for fertilizer himself.

Father Fiset's spiritual efforts were energetic and ambitious too. He organized the momentous job of building an enormous new stone church. The people of the community spent five years quarrying the stone on Chéticamp Island and hauling it across the ice each winter. The actual construction was a co-operative task as well, with all lumber being donated and each parishioner supplying one day of free labour each month. Costs, in spite of the donated services, totalled $41,950. In those days, the skilled masons from Quebec would have earned about $2.00 per day, and the labourers a mere 50 cents per day.

As well as the tradesmen, both the architect, D. Ouellet of Quebec City and the contractor, Hubert Morin of Trois-Pistoles, were from the province of Quebec. Perhaps for this reason, St. Peter's is so distinctly reminiscent of the large Roman Catholic churches in the small communities which dot

the shores of the St. Lawrence River. Like those Quebec counterparts, the massive St. Peter's has a shoreline setting, is Romanesque in style, and has the small dwellings of the village clustered about its base.

The exterior of the structure is solid and imposing, measuring 212 feet in length and 74 feet in width. The light brown freestone or sandstone, which is flecked with sparkling mica, is rusticated or rough-cut to add to the impression of rugged stability. In keeping with the Romanesque style, the windows and door openings are all round-headed and accented by arched label mouldings with prominent central keystones. The front façade is decorated with a pedimented gable and corner pilasters which finish in statuary. The central doorway and large round window above are set in a rectangular panel of smooth-cut stone; on each side the smaller doors and windows above are also highlighed by inset, arched panels of smooth-cut stone. Truncated triangular insets of smooth stone accent the pedimented gable and hipped roof.

The upper section of the stone tower has two front round-headed windows topped with stringcourse moulding with a centred keystone and classical pediments. The octagonal domed belfry is very decorative with pilaster detail, pediments above the open arches, and hooded dormers. The pointed spire rises above to a height of 180 feet. Both the belfry and spire have a stunning silver cladding.

The interior is probably the most highly ornamented interior of any church in the province. So lavish is the gilt-trimmed plasterwork that one might describe the style as Baroque. Three levels of arches, the wide arches at ground level, the classical, rounded arches of the side galleries, and the smaller recessed arches along the central ceiling arch, provide an inspiring rhythmic beauty. Even the gallery fronts are decorated with the classical arch motif to add to the basic rhythm of design. Everywhere there is rich embellishment, from the gilt-touched scrolls on the pillar capitals and the deeply moulded cornice work to the intricately patterned gold medallions which surround the gallery lights and the bas-relief shields which decorate the recessed ceiling arches. The rhythm of arches culminates in the gilt-edged frescoes and canopied ceiling behind the altar.

In spite of the opulence of the interior décor, there is no sense of gaudiness to mar the beauty, perhaps because of the tasteful colour scheme. Pastel shades of green and aqua are used with white and delicate gold leaf accents. The effect is wholly pleasing and unforgettable.

Repainting and redecorating has taken place twice during the history of the church, and proved to be costly both times. In 1919, the sum was $19,000 and in 1957, when the frescoes were added, the total reached $55,000. One hardly dares to calculate the escalation in prices since then, and even worse, what they may become when the next repainting occurs!

Presently directed by the Eudist Fathers, the parish of Chéticamp has remained the most francophone in Cape Breton. When visitors come to the scenic coastal community, they should stop to savour the Acadian culture. They will not fail to notice St. Peter's Church, the great stone church with its gleaming, silvered spire. And they should not fail to take time to see its magnificent interior.

St. John's, Strathlorne

One of the most picturesque churches in Cape Breton is St. John's United at Strathlorne. Situated in a wooded grove just off the main road to Inverness, this medium-sized rural church is truely a photographer's delight. The central subject, the church itself, is in pristine condition; the old clapboards gleam with fresh white paint and the decorative features are highlighted in shiny black paint.

The historical roots of the congregation date back to the early days of Presbyterianism in Cape Breton. The first settler in the valley of Strathlorne was John "Ban" MacLean from the Island of Rum, Scotland. He came about 1800, and sent such enthusiastic reports back to his friends and relatives that many of them joined him in the new land in 1810 or soon after.

For almost 30 years, there were probably no Presbyterian clergyman in the area, not even itinerant missionaries, for John "Ban" MacLean's first eight children were baptised by Roman Catholic priests. The two youngest children, born after 1828, were given Presbyterian baptisms. The first minister was Rev. Aeneas MacLean, who came in 1828, and made Strathlorne the centre of his missionary activities on Cape Breton Island.

The first church was built, in 1831, on the site of the present church and on land that was part of the farmland of John "Ban" MacLean, the original settler. On September 24, 1840, the Rev. John Gunn was ordained and inducted into the charge of Strathlorne; this marked the first ordination service held in Cape Breton by the Presbyterian Church. Rev. Gunn's mission field was very extensive, encompassing the Margaree Valley and stretching all the way to Pleasant Bay, Aspy Bay, and even Bay St. Lawrence on the northeastern tip of Cape Breton. During Rev. Gunn's 30-year ministry a second church was built in 1856.

It was during the 12-year term of Strathlorne's sixth minister, Rev. Dr. Donald MacDonald, that the present church was constructed, in 1895. Dr. MacDonald has been described as "a scholarly Evangelical preacher, a faithful and devoted pastor and most methodical in all his work." When the first manse was destroyed by fire and all the records lost, Dr. MacDonald collected material and reconstituted a record which was hailed as "a marvel of completeness."

With the opening of the coal mine in the town of Inverness, and the resulting influx in population, Dr. MacDonald's congregation rose from 165 families to over 200. The need for a larger church was evident. As well, a church hall was built in the town, which did not have its own Presbyterian church until about 1908.

Architecturally, St. John's is an excellent example of the blending of classical and Gothic elements so typical of rural Nova Scotia churches, particularly in Cape Breton. The configuration is symmetrical, with a central tower, and a window on either side of the main door. The classical symmetry is further emphasized by the prominent Gothic corner pilasters and finials. The tower is also ornamented with corner pilasters displaying Gothic motifs and caps. The belfry is decorated with sharply peaked gables and surmounted by an Early English style "broach" spire. Even the small knobs that finish the tops of the spire and corner finials are still intact, and contribute to the overall impression of symmetry.

The window, door and belfry openings are all Gothic, accented with narrow label mouldings. An unique feature, which must have been the inspiration of the local craftsmen, is the division of the windows to match the division between centre door and the window above. The creation of the intervening space allows room for the attractive, raised ornaments with quatre-foil motifs.

The interior is surprisingly spacious. The colourful tones of rose and the dark-stained wood of the ceiling create a warm atmosphere. While there is not a great deal of embellishment, the slender, Gothic windows along the sides have their characteristic label mouldings. The most stunning feature is the broad sweep of the curved gallery across the back of the church.

St. John's United at Strathlorne is well worth visiting, both as a fitting monument to the Presbyterian pioneers and for its own photogenic qualities.

First Baptist, Amherst

The town of Amherst in Cumberland County, near the New Brunswick border, has an individuality which is immediately visible in its architecture. Many of the public and commercial buildings are constructed of rich, red sandstone. The First Baptist Church is no exception; it is, indeed, an impressive example, a large, red sandstone structure, located beside the square at the town's centre, along with Christ Church Anglican and the courthouse.

Built in 1895, First Baptist Church is the third church on the site. The earliest years of the Baptist faith in Amherst were characterized by the visits made by itinerant New Light and Baptist preachers. One Baptist missionary, Rev. Joseph Crandall, of New Brunswick, eventually organized the Amherst Baptist congregation in 1809. The first church was built a decade later in 1819. It was a plain, 40-foot square meeting house which the Baptists shared with other protestant denominations which had contributed funds for its construction. In fact, a Board of ten trustees, six baptists and four from other sects, was set up to oversee the details of construction; a Finance committee of three baptists and two others administered the funds and looked after the maintenance of the building. The second church on the site was not ecumenical and belonged solely to the baptists, who had significantly increased their numbers to 212 by 1861. Built in 1863, the second church was a classical wooden structure with a square central tower and gothic windows. The building may not have been very stable, as, in 1876, the deacons instigated the removal of the steeple because it was endangering the framework of the structure. The precarious condition of the building and the fact that the membership again increased dramatically necessitated the construction of the present, third church.

Under the ministry of Dr. David Allen Steele, a noted scholar, author, and preacher, the size of the congregation grew to 315 in 1881, and to 508 by 1891. Dr. Steele wrote two histories of Amherst and numerous articles which appeared regularly in publications of the Baptist Church. He was keenly interested in education and served on both the Amherst Board of School Commissioners and the Board of Governors of Acadia University, where he himself had received his Bachelor, Master, and Doctor of Divinity degrees. Theological students who served an apprenticeship under him testified that one year with Dr. Steele was worth all their years of theological studies. Although Dr. Steele was not of robust health and was often in pain, he almost miraculously "filled each fleeting minute with sixty seconds worth of duty done." It was towards the end of his 29-year ministry to the First Baptist congregation that the major church building project was embarked upon.

In 1891, the church records indicate that discussion about a new church had begun, and by 1893, a business committee was appointed to secure plans, let tenders, and generally administer the construction details. The men who served on the committee were

Deacon Thomas R. Black, Nelson Rhodes, Matthew Pride, George W. Christie, James Moffat, William Read, and G.B. Smith. All were prominent in the commercial and industrial life of the town. The project was undertaken with the highest efficiency. On July 6, 1894, the cornerstone was laid by Miss Annie Hickman. A little more than one year later, in September 1895, the large, stone edifice had been completed at a cost of $30,000.

The red sandstone used in construction was from a quarry located within the town limits. The quarry, operated by the Amherst Red Stone Quarry Co. Ltd. was "well and favourably known among architects and builders." The beds, which were about 40 feet thick, yielded the rich sandstone that improved and hardened with age. The merits of the stone were recognized elsewhere; large quantities were shipped to Ottawa, Montreal, Toronto, Saint John and Halifax. The First Baptist Church of Amherst was said to be one of the buildings "where the stone is seen at its best." The contractor was the firm of Rhodes and Curry of Amherst, and the architect was H.H. Mott of Saint John, New Brunswick.

For First Baptist Church, the stone was not smooth-cut in large blocks. Instead it was rough-cut in varying sized pieces laid together in random coursing to give a rugged, medieval castle-like appearance. The structure is Gothic in design, measuring 122 feet by 70 feet, and has two round, asymmetrical turrets which are 100 and 75 feet in height, respectively.

It is interesting to note that while the Baptists usually used simple, Classical building styles in the rural areas, more lavish Gothic styles were chosen for urban centres. The use of an unsymmetrical form and two towers appears around the province, in the United Baptist churches of Lockeport on the South Shore, and Bridgetown in the Annapolis Valley. In Yarmouth, the two baptist churches, Temple United Baptist, built in 1870, and Zion United Baptist, built in 1895, both have two asymmetrical towers.

The windows of First Baptist are Gothic arches for the most part, with slim rectangular windows in the turrets. The corners of the main structure are decorated with Gothic buttresses and small, projecting hoodmoulds. The turrets are banded with stringcourse detailing and have ornamented doorways in a modified version of Early English Gothic style, which combined pointed arches with rounded pilaster decoration.

The interior has a vaulted Gothic ceiling supported by round columns with elaborate gold-painted capitals. Eleven years after the church was built, in 1906, the membership had risen to more than 800; to accommodate the influx, a large gallery, which curves around three sides of the nave and has a seating

capacity of 400, was constructed in 1907. In 1957, the Ralston Room with its perimeter classrooms was added, along with new boiler and storage rooms. In 1977, further interior renovations were carried out, including the construction of offices for the pastor, associate pastor, and secretary in part of the vestry.

Throughout the years, a number of sons and daughters of First Baptist Church have attained national and international prominence. Norman MacLeod Rogers, a Rhodes Scholar, history professor, and politician, served as the federal Minister of Labour and Minister of National Defence in the MacKenzie King government from 1935 to 1940. James Layton Ralston, lawyer, soldier, and statesman, rose to the rank of Colonel and won a D.S.O. in World War I; later he was Minister of National Defence and Minister of Finance under Prime Minister King.

The foremost member was Sir Charles Tupper, eldest son of Rev. Dr. Charles Tupper, the first resident pastor of First Baptist Church. Young Charles Tupper graduated as a medical doctor at 22 years of age and went on to become leader of the provincial Conservative Party and Premier of Nova Scotia in 1860. As a Father of Confederation, he led his province into Confederation in 1867 and in 1896 served as Prime Minister of Canada.

The earthy, red stones of First Baptist Church in Amherst are not only a notable architectural arrangement, but also embody a glorious past.

Eglise Ste-Marie, Church Point

COMEAU
PRECILLE

Perhaps more than any other structure in the province, Eglise Ste-Marie (St. Mary's Church) stands as the culmination of church architecture in the era. The imposing edifice, the largest wooden building in North America, is a striking landmark on Nova Scotia's French Shore in Digby County.

The first group of families to settle in the Church Point area arrived in 1769 after a long journey on foot from Massachusetts. They were Acadians who had suffered the ignominious deportation in the previous decade. The first rough chapel was built at Grosses Coques in 1774; it is said to have been rectangular in shape with two openings for windows, one door, and walls "covered with irregularly-joined planks." A second chapel, similar in construction to the first, was built in 1786, on a point of land which juts out into St. Mary's Bay — hence the name Church Point.

When Father Jean-Mandé Sigogne, the first resident Roman Catholic priest, came a third church was erected on a more convenient site along the main road in the community. On September 10, 1820, fire swept through the area levelling 18 houses and 23 barns as well as the rectory and the church. By 1829, the church had been rebuilt; it was a large structure in the classical Georgian style of St. Paul's in Halifax. This church, named St. Mary's, served the parish until the present St. Mary's was opened in 1905.

The grand St. Mary's was the tangible realization of one man's dream. Father Pierre-Marie Dagnaud was born in Brittany, France, in 1858. The son of a carpenter, he was orphaned at the age of 12 years. In attending the Eudist seminary school, the young Pierre-Marie showed an exceptional aptitude for mathematics, a talent that later proved very useful for supervising the construction of the great church. He was ordained to the priesthood in 1882, and appointed head of Collège Ste-Anne in 1899. As head of the college he automatically became the parish priest of St. Mary's.

Father Dagnaud probably had no hesitation in choosing Auguste Regneault of Rennes, France, as architect. Mr. Regneault was the brother of the Assistant-General of the Eudist fathers and undoubtedly known to Father Dagnaud. The unique exterior design drew its inspiration from two notable sources. Firstly, the silhouette of the church, with its lofty spire, large side transepts and chancel extension, recalls the general impression of the church in Father Dagnaud's native village of Bains-sur-Ouste in France. Secondly, the architect, whose home in Rennes, France, was close to the famous chateaux of the Loire Valley, was surely influenced by their distinctive architecture.

That influence is shown directly by the use of various turrets on St. Mary's Church. Two large turrets flank the central steeple and four small turrets are placed at the base of the roof spire, giving the church a castle-like appearance. The two-storey, five-sided chancel extension is also very much a part of the French architectural tradition, particularly that of Auvergne in central France.

The Romanesque windows with label mouldings, which appear in pairs along the sides of the church, are attractive ornaments yet plain enough to allow a touch of rural simplicity to the grand edifice. Long, double, Romanesque belfry openings reinforce the window style, and a large, single, round-headed window decorates the tower. The rectangular windows in the turrets and banded across the centre of the tower accent the military or "chateau" style of the church.

The overall scale of St. Mary's Church is grandiose. The nave measures 190 feet in length while the transepts are 135 feet long. The width of the nave is 85 feet, and the height of the exterior walls, from the foundation to the roof, is 70 feet. The spire reaches a height of 185 feet which is approximately 27 feet lower than its original height. In the autumn of 1914, the steeple was struck by lightning during a raging storm; miraculously, as soon as the top of the spire burst into flames, the clouds opened and rain poured down, quenching the fire. During repairs, the burnt top was cut off and the spire refinished at a slightly lower height. Of three bronze bells, the largest weighs 1724 pounds, and 40 tons of stone act as ballast in the steeple.

Perhaps the most startling fact about the church, when one contemplates its lofty grandeur, is that its local builder, Léo Melanson of Little Brook, could not read or write. And yet, it was he who adapted and executed the plans of the French architect. His practical experience and natural talent as a master carpenter must have been immense. His confidence in his own ability was an important factor. One day he showed that confidence when asked if he was afraid the wind would blow the large steeple down. He replied, "Non, parce que c'est moi qui l'a fait (No, because I've made it myself)."

The interior of St. Mary's is as impressive as any of the great European cathedrals. The high, vaulted ceiling lit by the row of clerestory windows, the magnificent Romanesque arches supported by huge round pillars with ornate Corinthian capitals, and the sheer size of the nave and transepts, all combine to give the viewer an overpowering feeling of awe. The beauty of the décor, which reaches an almost heavenly splendor, is due in part to the bright expanse of pure white walls and restrained embellishment. Below the clerestory windows a band of ornamental Romanesque arches runs around the entire perimeter of the church, and nine delicate, flower-edged tableaux, done by Montreal artist L. St. Hilaire, are found on the central ceiling vaults.

Originally the parishioners sat on chairs as is the European custom, but in 1969, the chairs were replaced by white oak pews made in Shelburne, Nova Scotia. The three coal furnaces that heated the 13,481,000 cubic feet of space with some difficulty were exchanged in 1961 for a more efficient oil furnace.

The ordinary maintenance of a building of such enormous proportions is no small task. The first major repairs occurred in 1938 when the shingles were replaced on the south side of the main roof; 1946 saw the reshingling of the north side. In 1976, reshingling of the roofs

was again undertaken along with the renewal of all the flashings around the major windows and at the junctions of the various roof levels. The number of shingles required was an incredible 240,000! Perhaps the most harrowing repair job was the replacing of shingles on the high roofs of the steeple. Many of the shingles had begun to blow off with each heavy wind. The breathtakingly dangerous task was accomplished between April and October of 1979 at an estimated cost of $40,000.

Repainting of the interior, also a costly and difficult job, has only been done twice during the church's history. In 1946, a huge scaffolding on wheels was constructed so that it could be moved from section to section of the high vaulted ceiling. There was such a thickness of smoke and grime on the walls from the old coal furnaces that the whole interior had to be washed down before the painting could begin. In 1977, when the interior was again redecorated, 400 gallons of paint were used for the two coats on the walls and ceiling. At that time, the ceiling paintings and the statues were also retouched, while the woodwork, including the vast floor, was revarnished.

In order to pay hommage to all the workers, both those who built the church and those who have helped maintain it at great personal risk, the first Sunday of September has been set apart as a day of thanks. But an even more fitting tribute is the church itself, an architectural wonder and a triumphant symbol of the rich Acadian culture in Nova Scotia.

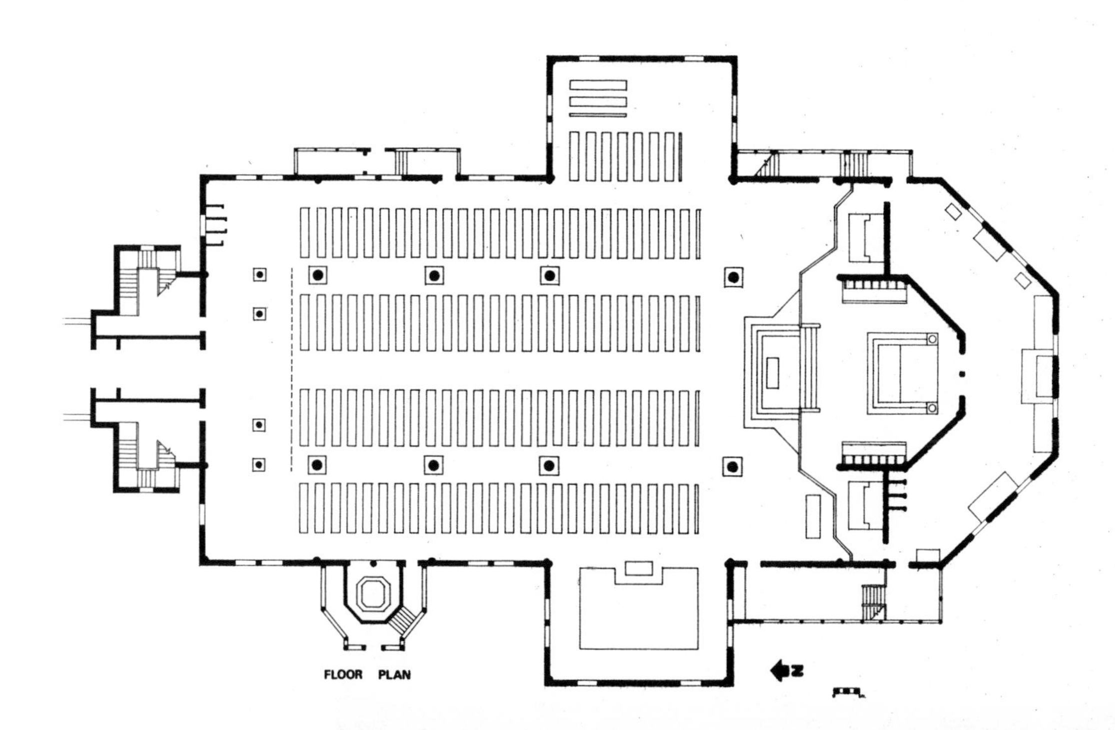

APPENDIX AND GLOSSARY

Appendix

A county by county listing of the 577 churches surveyed follows. Along with churches from the 1830 to 1910 period, the listing includes 28 from the earlier 1750 to 1830 period as this volume completes the study begun in the companion volume, *Thy Dwellings Fair*. The churches are identified by the name and/or denomination, and place. The architectural style of each church is noted under four categories according to the following key.

Key

1. **Configuration**
   S symmetrical
   U unsymmetrical
2. **Steeple Position or Type**
   C centre position
   D double or two steeples
   S side position
   B small bell-cote
3. **Window Type**
   c classical or round-headed
   g Gothic or pointed
   r rectilinear
4. **Detailing**
   c classical
   g Gothic

The first capital letter within the brackets denotes the general configuration. If a second capital letter appears, it indicates the position or type of steeple. If a second capital letter is not used, there is no steeple on the church. The first lower case letter classifies the type of window, and the second lower case letter indicates the style of detailing. If a second lower case letter does not appear, then the style of detailing is the same as the style of the window type.

In some cases, churches have been changed over the years; steeples have been added or removed, for instance. While these changes have been taken into account in assessing regional designs, only the present form of the churches is shown in this listing.

Annapolis
Deep Brook United Baptist (USrc); St. Matthew's Anglican, Deep Brook (SCgc); St. Edward's Anglican, Clementsport (USg); Old St. Edward's, Clementsport (SCc); Clementsport Baptist (SBg); Clementsport United (SCg); Goat Island Baptist (SCgc); St. Luke's, Annapolis Royal (SCgc); Annapolis Royal United Baptist (USg); Christ Church, Karsdale (SCgc); Granville Ferry United Baptist (SCrc); Granville Ferry United Church (USg); Holy Trinity, Granville Ferry (USg); All Saints, Granville Centre (SCc); United Baptist, Granville Centre (USg); Centenary United (Ug); Bridgetown United (USg); St. James Anglican, Bridgetown (USg); Bridgetown United Baptist (UDg); Paradise Baptist (USg); St. Andrew's Anglican, Lawrencetown (SCgc); Lawrencetown United (USg); Clarence United Baptist (SCgc); Wilmot Mountain Baptist, Mount Rose (Sgc); Mount Hanley Baptist (Sgc); Port George United Baptist (SCgc); Margaretsville United Baptist (SCg); Margaretsville United (SCgc); Evergreen United Baptist, Margaretsville (Sgc); Presbyterian Church, Melvern Square (Sg); Melvern Square United Baptist (SCgc); Old Holy Trinity, Middleton (SCrc); Holy Trinity Anglican, Middleton (UBg); Middleton United Baptist (USc); St. John's United, Middleton (Sg); Wilmot Union Church (SCgc); Granville Beach Baptist (Src).

Antigonish
St. Ninian's Roman Catholic, Antigonish (SDc); St. James United, Antigonish (SCgc); Chapel of St. Paul The Apostle, Antigonish (UCg); St. Patrick's Roman Catholic, Lochaber Lake (SCgc); St. David's United, Cape George (SCg); Our Lady of the Rosary, Cape George (SCg); St. George's Roman Catholic, Georgeville (SCg); St. Margaret's Roman Catholic, Arisaig (SCg); St. Peter's Roman Catholic, Tracadie (SCgc); Holy Cross Roman Catholic, Pomquet (SCgc).

Cape Breton
Big Pond Roman Catholic (SCg); St. Mary's Roman Catholic, East Bay (SCgc); Sacred Heart Roman Catholic, Sydney (UDg); St. Patrick's, Sydney (SCg); St. George's Anglican, Sydney (SCg); South Bar Baptist (Sg); St. Paul's Presbyterian, Glace Bay (UDc); Glace Bay United Baptist (UDg); Glace Bay Synagogue (Sg); St. John's United, Port Morien (USg); Zion Presbyterian, Louisbourg (USr); St.

Bartholomew's Anglican, Louisbourg (USg); Union Presbyterian, Albert Bridge (SCgc); St. Columba Presbyterian, Marion Bridge (SCgc); St. Columba United, Leitches Creek (SCc); St. Joseph's Roman Catholic, North Sydney (USg); Calvary Baptist, North Sydney (USc); St. Andrew's Presbyterian, Sydney Mines (USg); Sydney Mines Roman Catholic (SCg); Trinity Anglican, Sydney Mines (USg); Clyde Avenue United Baptist, Sydney Mines (USg); Carmen United, Sydney Mines (UDg); Mitchell's Island Union Church, Point Edward (SCrc); St. John the Evangelist, Point Edward (SCg).

Colchester

Union Church, Bayhead (Sgc); Sharon United, Tatamagouche (SCgc); The Falls Presbyterian (Src); Knox Presbyterian, Earltown (SCgc); United Baptist, Nuttby (Sg); Aenon Baptist, North River (Src); St. John The Evangelist, Truro (USg); Immanuel Baptist, Truro (USr); Bass River United (SCr); Bass River United Baptist (SCr); St. James' United, Great Village (SCg); Peniel United, Five Islands (SCg); Christ Church Anglican, Clifton (SCgc); Old Barns United (SCg).

Cumberland

St. James' Presbyterian, Oxford (Sgc); Trinity United, Oxford (USgc); Oxford United Baptist (USc); All Souls' Anglican, Oxford (Ug); St. Andrew's United, Oxford Junction (Sc); Oxford Junction Anglican (Ug); River Philip United (SCc); St. John's Roman Catholic, Springhill (SDc); All Saints' Anglican, Springhill (USg); First Baptist, Amherst (UDg); Trinity-St. Stephen's United, Amherst (USg); Christ Church Anglican, Amherst (UCg); St. Charles Roman Catholic, Amherst (UDc); Amherst Point Baptist Church (Src); Church of the Good Shepherd, Tidnish (USg); Lorneville United (SCgc); Calvary United, Port Philip (Sr); Wesley-St. Matthew's United, Pugwash (SCgc); St. Thomas More Roman Catholic, Pugwash (SCc); Melville United, Gulf Shore (SCgc); Wallace Bridge Baptist (USrc); St. Andrew's Anglican, Wallace (UBg); St. John's United, Wallace (USg); Holy Trinity, Port Grenville (USg); Parrsboro United Baptist (SCg); St. Brigid's Roman Catholic, Parrsboro (SCg); St. Mark's Anglican, Moose River (USg); St. John's Anglican, Diligent River (USg).

Digby

Eglise Sacré-Coeur, Saulnierville (SCg); St. Mary's, Church Point (SCcg); St. Bernard's, St. Bernard (SDg); St. Joseph's Roman Catholic, Weymouth (SCgc); St. Thomas Anglican, Weymouth (SCgc); St. Peter's Anglican, Weymouth North (USg); Weymouth North Baptist (SCg); St. Mary's Bay United Baptist (SCg); All Saints' Anglican, Rossway (SCgc); Rossway United Baptist (Sg); Digby Neck First United Baptist, Centreville (SCg); Church of the Nativity, Sandy Cove (SCrc); Sandy Cove United Baptist (SCrc); Tiverton Christian Church (SCc); Freeport United Baptist (Src); Westport United Baptist (SCgc); Westport Church of Christ Disciples (SCg); Little River United Baptist (SCgc); Digby United Baptist (USg); Grace United, Digby (SCgc); Trinity Anglican, Digby (USg); Bear River United Baptist (SCgc); Hillsborough United, Bear River (SCgc); St. Anne's Roman Catholic, Bear River (Src); Landsdowne Baptist (Sg); Smith's Cove Methodist (SCg); Old Baptist Meeting House, Smith's Cove (Sgc); Smith's Cove United Baptist (SCg); Hill Grove United Baptist, Acaciaville (SCgc).

Guysborough

St. Andrew's Anglican Mulgrave (USg); St. James' Anglican, Middle Melford (USg); Hadleyville United (Src); Holy Trinity Anglican, Hadleyville (USg); Manchester United (Sc); St. Paul's Anglican, Boylston (USg); Boylston United Baptist (SCgc); Boylston United (SCg); Wesley United, Guysborough (SCgc); St. Ann's Roman Catholic, Guysborough (SCgc); Christ Church Anglican, Guysborough (SCg); Guysborough United Baptist (USg); St. James' Anglican, Halfway Cove (SCg); St. Vincent de Paul, Queensport (SCg); Queensport United Baptist (SCr); All Saints' Anglican, Canso (USg); Star of the Sea Roman Catholic, Canso (SCg); St. Paul's United, Canso (USrg); Canso United Baptist (USg); Grace United, White Head (SCrc); Port Felix Roman Catholic (SCg); St. Bartholomew's Anglican, Cole Harbour (SCg); St. Joseph's Roman Catholic, Charlos Cove (SCg); New Harbour United (SCrc); New Harbour United Baptist (SCgc); Seal Harbour United Baptist (SCr); Goldboro Baptist (USc); Isaac's Harbour Baptist (SCg); Stormont Union Church (SCg); Holy Trinity Anglican, Country Harbour (SCg); Zion United, Country Harbour (SCgc); United Baptist, Country Harbour (SCr); Kirk Memorial United, Aspen (SCgc); St. John's United, Sherbrooke (USr); St. James' Presbyterian, Sherbrooke (SCr); St. James' Anglican, Sherbrooke (SCgc); Goldenville Church (USg); St. John's United, Liscomb (SCg); St. Luke's Anglican, Liscomb (SCg); St. Matthew's Anglican, Marie Joseph (USg); St. Barnabas Anglican, Ecum Secum (SCg).

Halifax

Necum Teuch Anglican (USg); St. Mary's Anglican, Moosehead (USg); St. Giles Presbyterian, Moser River (USg); St. James' Anglican, Port Dufferin (USg); St. James' United, Port Dufferin (USg); St. Andrew's Anglican, Watt Section (USg); St. James' United, Sheet Harbour (SCg); St. Peter's, Sheet Harbour (SCc); St. James' Anglican, Spry Bay (UCg); St. James United, Spry Bay (SCr); St. Andrew's Anglican, Spry Harbour (USg); Pope's Harbour United (SCr); St. Martin's Roman Catholic, Tangier (SCg); Holy Trinity Anglican, Tangier (USg); St. Thomas' Anglican, Mooseland (USg); St. Peter's Anglican, Murphy's Cove (USg); St. Denis Roman Catholic, East Ship Harbour (USg); St. Stephen's Anglican, Ship Harbour (USg); Gay's River United (SCrg); St. Andrew's United, Elderbank (SCg); St. James' United, Upper Musquodoboit (SCg); St. John's Anglican, Oyster Pond (USg); Oyster Pond United (SBg); St. Thomas Anglican, Musquodoboit Harbour (SCrg); St. Barnabas Anglican, Head Chezzetcook (SCg); St. John's Anglican, Westphal (UBg); St. James' United, Dartmouth (SCg); Victoria Road Baptist, Dartmouth (Uc); Christ Church, Dartmouth (SCc); St. Paul's Anglican, Halifax (SCc); Little Dutch Church, Halifax (SCr); St. George's Anglican, Halifax (SCrc); St. Mary's Basilica, Halifax (SCg); Our Lady of Sorrows, Halifax (SCg); St. Matthew's United, Halifax (SCg); St. David's Presbyterian, Halifax (Sg); Fort Massey United, Halifax (USg); Cornwallis Street Baptist, Halifax (USc); St. Patrick's Roman Catholic, Halifax (SCg); St. John's Anglican, Sackville (SCg); Cole Harbour Meeting House (Sg); Sambro United (SCg); St. Peter's Roman Catholic, Ketch Harbour (USg); St. Peter's Anglican, Hackett's Cove (USg); Stella Maris, Ferguson's Cove (SDc); William Black Memorial, Glen Margaret (SCc); St. Margaret's Anglican, Tantallon (UBg); St. James Anglican, Boutilier's Point (UBg); United Baptist, Head St. Margaret's Bay (SCg); St. John's Anglican, Peggy's Cove (USg); All Saints' Anglican, Bedford (USg).

Hants

Church of the Holy Spirit, Lakelands (SCg); South Rawdon United Baptist (USg); St. Paul's Anglican, Rawdon (SCgc); Newport United (SCgc); St. James' Anglican, Brooklyn (USg); St. Croix United (SCrc); Juniper Grove United, Falmouth (SCg); Falmouth United Baptist (SCg); United Baptist, Windsor (USg); St. John's Roman Catholic, Windsor (USg); Christ Church, Windsor (USg); St. John's United, Windsor (USg); King's College Chapel, Windsor (UBg);

Burlington United (USg); Kempt Shore United (SCgc); Cheverie United (U); Bramber United Baptist (SCgc); Cambridge United Baptist (SCr); Pembroke United (SCgc); Walton Anglican (Ug); Noel United (SCrc); Lower Selma Meeting House (Sc); Selma United (SCg); Holy Trinity Anglican, Maitland (UBg); St. David's United, Maitland (SCc); St. Andrew's Anglican, Hantsport (USg); Hantsport United Baptist (SCgc); Mount Denson United (SCgc).

Inverness
Stewart United, Whycocomagh (SCg); St. Joseph's Roman Catholic, Glencoe Mills (SBg); Hillsborough United, Mabou (SCg); St. Mary's Roman Catholic, Mabou (SCg); St. Stephen's United, Port Hood (USg); St. John's United, Strathlorne (SCg); St. Matthew's United, Inverness (UDg); Stella Maris Roman Catholic, Inverness (SDc); St. Margaret's Roman Catholic, Broad Cove (SCg); St. Patrick's Roman Catholic, North East Margaree (SCg); Wilson United, Margaree Centre (SCg); Big Intervale United (Sr); Eglise St. Joseph, St. Joseph du Moine (SCg); Eglise St. Pierre, Cheticamp (SCc); Jerseymen's Church, Cheticamp (SCg); St. David's United, Port Hastings (USg); Stella Maris Roman Catholic, Creignish (SCc); St. Margaret of Scotland, River Denys Mountain (SCc); St. Mary's of the Angels, Glendale (SCgc).

Kings
Star of the Sea Roman Catholic, Morden (Sg); Christ Church Anglican, Morden (USg); Morden United (Src); Harbourville United (SCg); St. Mary's Auburn (SCc); Berwick Baptist (SCgc); Christ Church, Berwick (UBgc); Cambridge Baptist (USgc); Billtown United Baptist (USrg); West Hall's Harbour Baptist (Src); Aylesford United (USc); Greenwich United (USgc); Port Williams United Baptist (SCgc); Church of Saint John, Cornwallis (SCc); Trinity United, Canning (USgc); St. John's Anglican, Wolfville (UBg); St. Francis of Assisi, Wolfville (Sgc); Old Covenanter Church, Grand Pré (USrc).

Lunenburg
St. James' Anglican, Mahone Bay (USg); St. John's Lutheran, Mahone Bay (SCg); Trinity United, Mahone Bay (SCg); United Baptist, Mahone Bay (SCg); Calvary Temple, Mahone Bay (USg); Zion Lutheran, Lunenburg (UDg); Central United, Lunenburg (USg); St. Andrew's Presbyterian, Lunenburg (SCg); St.

Norbert's Roman Catholic, Lunenburg (SCg); St. John's Anglican, Lunenburg SCg); Grace Lutheran, First South (USg); First South United (SCr); St. Matthew's Evangelical Lutheran, Rose Bay (USg); St. Andrew's Presbyterian, Rose Bay (SCg); Trinity United, Rose Bay (UDg); St. Mark's Lutheran, Middle LaHave (USg); St. Bartholomew's Anglican, Middle LaHave (SC); St. John's United, Middle LaHave (USc); St. Matthew's Anglican, Upper LaHave (USg); Mt. Olivet Evangelical Lutheran, Upper LaHave (USg); Dayspring Baptist (SCg); St. Augustine's Anglican, Conquerall Bank (SBg); Conquerall Mills Church (Sg); St. Peter's Anglican, West LaHave (USg); LaHave United (Sr); St. James' Anglican, LaHave (USg); Knox Presbyterian, Dublin Shore (USg); West Dublin United (USg); St. Matthew's Presbyterian, West Dublin (USg); St. John's Anglican, West Dublin (USg); St. Michael's Anglican, Petite Riviere (USg); Wesley United, Petite Riviere (SCr); St. Matthew's United, Broad Cove (USgc); St. Mark's Anglican, Broad Cove (USc); St. Paul's Anglican, Cherry Hill (USg); Vogler's Cove United (USg); Calvary Lutheran, Middlewood (USg); St. Luke's Lutheran, Baker's Settlement (USg); Hemford Church (SCg); Union Church, Simpson's Corner (SCr); St. John in the Wilderness, New Germany (SCg); Epworth United, New Germany (USr); Trinity Lutheran, New Germany (USg); New West Pine United, Pinehurst (SCg); St. Andrew's Lutheran, West Northfield (USg) St. Andrew's Anglican, West Northfield (SCr); Holy Trinity Anglican, Bridgewater (Ug); St. Joseph's Roman Catholic, Bridgewater (USg); St. Paul's Lutheran, Bridgewater (USg); Martin's River Church (SCg); St. Mark's Anglican, Western Shore (SCg); Christ Church, New Ross (UBg); St. Patrick's, New Ross (SCg).

Pictou

St. Mary's Roman Catholic, Lismore (SCgc); St. Paul's Presbyterian, Merigomish (SCg); St. Andrew's Roman Catholic, Egerton (SCg); Zion Presbyterian, Eureka (SCg); First Presbyterian, Hopewell (SCrc); St. Columba, Hopewell (Src); Christ Church, Stellarton (SCg); St. John's, MacLennan's Mountain (Src); Springville Presbyterian (Src); St. Paul's Presbyterian, St. Paul (Src); Blair Presbyterian, Garden of Eden (Src); Bethel Church, Caledonia (Src); Calvin Church, Sunnybrae (Src); St. Andrew's Presbyterian, Gairloch (SCgc); Sutherland's River Presbyterian (SCr); Salem Presbyterian, Greenhill (Sg); Zion Presbyterian, East River St. Mary's (SCg); West River Presbyterian, Durham (SCrc); Westminster

Presbyterian, New Glasgow (USg); St. Andrew's (Kirk) Church, New Glasgow (SCgc); First United Baptist, New Glasgow (UScg); Our Lady of Lourdes, Stellarton (SCg); Union Presbyterian, Thorburn (SCrg); St. Ann's Roman Catholic, Thorburn (SCg); St. Luke's Presbyterian, Salt Springs (SCg); Knox Presbyterian, Blue Mountain (USg); First Presbyterian, Pictou (SCg); St. Andrew's Presbyterian, Pictou (SCg); Stella Maris Roman Catholic, Pictou (SCg); St. Andrew's Presbyterian, Westville (UDrg); St. David's Presbyterian, Toney River (Src); St. John's Anglican, River John (USg); St. George's Presbyterian, River John (SCrc); Salem United, River John (SCg); West Branch United (SCg).

Queen's
Bethany United, Mill Village (USg); All Saints' Anglican, Mill Village (UBg); Port Medway United Baptist (SCr); Church of Holy Redeemer Anglican, Port Medway (UBg); Old Meeting House, Port Medway (Sr); Emmanuel United, Port Medway (USg); Pilgrim United, Brooklyn (USg); Brooklyn Baptist (SCc); Trinity Anglican, Liverpool (UCg); St. Gregory's Roman Catholic, Liverpool (SCc); Liverpool United Baptist (SCg); Zion United, Liverpool (SCg); Summerville Christian Church (USg); Port Mouton United (USg); Port Mouton United Baptist (SCrc).

Richmond
Cleveland United (SCg); Black River United, Dundee (SCr); L'Assomption, Arichat (SDcg); Eglise St. Joseph, Petit de Grat (SCg); Eglise St. Jean-Baptiste, River Bougeois (SCg); United Church, St. Peter's (USg); Church of Immaculate Conception, Simon River (SCgc); Sacred Heart Roman Catholic, Johnstown (SCg).

Shelburne
Sable River United Baptist (USg); Louis Head United Baptist (SCg); Little Harbour United (USg); Ragged Island Baptist (SCc); Lockeport United Baptist (UDg); Lockeport United (Sg); Holy Cross Anglican, Lockeport (UBg); East Jordan Union Church (SBg); Jordan Falls United Baptist (USg); Holy Trinity Anglican, Jordan Falls (USg); Jordan Ferry Union Church (SCg); Lower Sandy Point Baptist (USrg); St. Peter's By the Sea Anglican, Sandy Point (UCg); Hope Wesleyan, Sandy Point (USg); Trinity United, Shelburne (USg); Shelburne

United Baptist (SCgc); Trinity United, Northeast Harbour (USr); Bethany United, Ingomar (USg); St. Paul's United, Carleton Village (SCrc); St. Matthew's United, Clyde River (SCg); Port Clyde United (SCg); Upper Port LaTour United (USr); Port LaTour United Baptist (SBg); Wesley United, Barrington (SCc); Temple United Baptist, Barrington (SCg); Old Meeting House, Barrington (Sr); St. James' United, Barrington Passage (SCgc); South Side United Baptist (USr); Doctor's Cove United Baptist (SCr); Atwood's Brook Church (SCg); Chapel Hill Museum Church (SCgc); Wood's Harbour Church (SCc).

Victoria
Cape North United (SCgc); First Presbyterian, Cape North (SCc); Aspy Bay United (Ugc); St. Andrew's United, Bay St. Lawrence (SCr); St. Peter's Presbyterian, Neil's Harbour (SCgc); Calvin Presbyterian, Birch Plain (SCg); St. Andrew's Presbyterian, North River Bridge (SCg); Ephraim Scott Memorial Presbyterian, South Gut St. Ann's (SCgc); Greenwood United, Baddeck (USg); St. Peter's & St. John's Anglican, Baddeck (USg); St. Andrew's United, Baddeck Forks (Src); Farquharson Memorial Presbyterian, Middle River (SCgc).

Yarmouth
Eglise de l'Immaculée Conception, Middle East Pubnico (SCcg); Eglise Saint Pierre, Middle West Pubnico (SCg); Glenwood United Baptist (SCc); Sainte Anne, Ste-Anne-du-Ruisseau (SDc); St. Stephen's Anglican, Tusket (USg); Tusket United Church (USg); Pleasant Lake United Baptist (Sg); Arcadia United (USgc); Arcadia United Baptist (SCc); Plymouth United Baptist (Sr); Saint Raphael, Pinkney Point (SCr); Eglise Saint-Joseph, Ile Surette (SCc); Sainte-Agnès, Quinan (SCg); Buttes-Amirault Roman Catholic (UDc); Central Cheboque United Baptist (Src); Cheboque United (SCc); Rockville United Baptist (SCrc); Temple United Baptist, Yarmouth (UDg); Zion United Baptist, Yarmouth (UDc); Holy Trinity Anglican, Yarmouth (USg); St. Ambrose Cathedral, Yarmouth (SCc); Jewish Synagogue, Yarmouth (SCg); Mountain Cemetery Chapel, Yarmouth (SCg); Bayview United Baptist, Port Maitland (Ugc); Beaver River United Baptist (SCgc); Gavelton United Baptist (Src).

Glossary

Board and batten: vertical wooden cladding of wide boards and narrow strips which cover joints between the boards.

Capital: the top of a column.

Clerestory: upper portion of church walls which are pierced by windows.

Dentil: small teeth-like blocks found under a cornice or the eaves of a building.

Entablature: the horizontal segment above the capitals of classical columns.

Finial: a spiked ornament at the top of a spire, gable, pediment or other point.

Gable: a triangular top of an end wall, doorway, etc.

Label: moulding around the top of a window or door extending part way down each side.

Moulding: a continuous linear or lined ornament.

Mullion: the upright part of window tracery.

Muntins: the narrow strips of wood between panes of glass in a window.

Pediment: a triangular part used above doors, windows or porches.

Pilaster: a column or half-column ornament projecting slightly from a wall.

Return: a horizontal continuation of a moulding at the corner of a building.

Stringcourse: a projecting horizontal band of moulding around a building.

BIBLIOGRAPHY
AND
CREDITS

Bibliography

Regional Design

Pevsner, Nikolaus, *An Outline of European Architecture*, Penguin Books Ltd., Harmondsworth, Middlesex, England, 1960 Edition.

Sellman, R.R., *English Churches*, Methuen & Co. Ltd., London, England.

Harries, John, *Discovering Churches*, Shire Publications Ltd., Aylesbury, England, 1972.

Humphreys, Barbara, Meredith Sykes, *The Buildings of Canada, A guide to pre-20th-century styles in houses, churches and other structures*, Parks Canada and The Reader's Digest Association (Canada) Ltd., 1980.

The Illustrated Library of The World and Its People, 3 vols. United Kingdom, France II, Germany I, Greystone Press, New York, 1963.

Wallace, William et al., *250 Years Young, Our Diocesan Story 1710-1960*, published by The Anglican Diocese of Nova Scotia, 1960.

Coverstone, Jean L., *Church Architecture in Nova Scotia from 1750-1867*, a thesis submitted to the University of Indiana, 1972.

Churches

Casgrain, H.R., Centenaire de la mort du Père Jean-Mandé Sigogne, missionaire de la baie Sainte-Marie et premier curé de la paroisse Sainte-Marie (1844-1944) Yarmouth, The Lawson Publishing Co. Ltd., 1944.

Davis, Marilyn, "Father Jean M. Sigogne — Apostle to Acadians," The Chronicle-Herald, March 4, 1966.

Wiswall, Judge P., Letter regarding the Indian Settlement at Bear River, October 22, 1828.

Wiswall, Judge P., Letter regarding the Indian Chapel at Bear River, February 12, 1830.

Wiswall, Judge P., Abbé J.-M. Sigogne, Original Accounts for building of Indian Chapel, February 26, 1831 to October 14, 1831.

Mewse, Andrew, Subscription List for the Indian Chapel at Bear River, Annapolis County.

Farnham, William, Estimate and Bill of Scantling for Indian Chapel.

Johnston, Angus Anthony, *A History of the Catholic Church in Eastern Nova Scotia, Volume II-1827-1880*, St. Francis Xavier University Press, Antigonish, 1971.

"Corpus Christi Procession at Bailey's Brook," The Casket, June 14, 1860.

Hill, Rev. George W., *Records of the Church of England in Rawdon from Its Origin until the Present Date*, James Bowes and Sons, 1858.

Book of Records of St. Paul's Parish, Rawdon, N.S., pp. 26-29.

Gibson, M. Allen, "St. Paul's Anglican Church, Rawdon," The Chronicle-Herald, October 20, 1956.

"Established 1794," The Hants Journal, December 5, 1947.

History of St. Paul's Church, Rawdon, N.S., a manuscript included with the church records and published in The Diocesan Times, September and October, 1946.

"1850 — St. James' Church, Sherbrooke, N.S. — 1950," The Diocesan Times, October 1950.

"St. James' Church, Sherbrooke, N.S.," The Diocesan Times, January 1948.

"St. James Anglican Church, Sherbrooke, N.S.," a short anonymous manuscript, September 1973.

The Third Report of the Halifax Association in aid of the Colonial Church Society, pp. 20, 21, 27, 28, Halifax, 1850.

The Fifth Report of the Halifax Association in aid of the Colonial Church Society, pp. 20, 21, 22, 23, Halifax, 1852.

"Sherbrooke Village," a pamphlet published by the Nova Scotia Museum.

Leonard, Vernon B., *History of the Building in 1853 of the Clarence United Baptist Church*, a booklet published by the church, 1953.

Leonard, Margaret, *Historic Sketch of the Paradise-Clarence United Baptist Church 1810-1960*, a booklet published by the church, 1960.

MacIsaac, Margaret, editor, *St. Margaret's Church 1857-1982*, a book published by the church, 1982.

Hawkins, Marjorie, Hector L. MacKenzie, and John MacQuarrie, *Gairloch, Pictou County, Nova Scotia*, St. Andrew's, 1977.

Gibson, M. Allen, "St. Andrew's Presbyterian Church, Gairloch," The Chronicle-Herald, August 9, 1962.

Murray, Walter C., "History of St. Matthew's Church, Halifax, N.S.," Collections of the Nova Scotia Historical Society, Volume 16 pp. 137-171.

Hattie, R.M., *Looking Backward Over Two Centuries: An Historical Paper dealing with Certain Phases of the History of St. Matthew's Church, Halifax, N.S.*, Presented Under Auspices of the Kirk-Session and St. Matthew's Historical Society, November 24, 1944.

Gibson, M. Allen, "St. Matthew's United Church, Halifax," The Chronicle-Herald, July 29, 1961.

"St. Matthew's United Church," The Mail Star, November 27, 1965.

Bird, Will R., "Interesting Items Regarding St. Matthew's Church," from a pamphlet "St. Matthew's United Church of Canada," published by St. Matthew's.

"Oldest United Church Congregation to Celebrate 188th Anniversary On Sunday," The Halifax Mail, November 27, 1937.

Perry, Margaret L., "The Founding of St. Matthew's," The Atlantic Advocate, November 1974.

"The Passing Years," The Chronicle-Herald, July 24, 1959.

Dennis, William, "The First Protestant Dissenting Church In The Dominion Is The Historical Congregation of St. Matthew's, Halifax," The Halifax Herald, April 18, 1896.

"Replacing Window," The Mail-Star, July 7, 1953.

"Unusual Find In Steeple At St. Matthew's Church," The Mail-Star, August 7, 1959.

The Novascotian, January 12, 1857, p. 3; January 19, 1857, p. 2; September 19, 1859, p. 3.

The Acadian Recorder, May 15, 1858, p. 2; May 17, 1858, p. 2; October 9, 1877, p. 3.

The Morning Sun, October 28, 1859, p. 2; May 20, 1859, p. 2; November 8, 1858, p. 2; May 12, 1858, p. 2; January 8, 1857, p. 2.

The Morning Journal, September 4, 1857, p. 3.

The British Colonist, August 9, 1859, p. 2.

"Laying of the Cornerstone of the new St. Matthew's Church," *St. Matthew's Session Records 1852-1882*, June 18, 1858.

Looking Backward Over Two Centuries: A Short History of St. Matthew's United Church, Halifax, N.S., from the Founding of the City to the Bicentenary Year, United Church of Canada, 1949.

St. Matthew's Church Records, entries from September 22, 1857 to March 10, 1860.

McInnis, Henry, "St. John's Presbyterian Church, MacLennan's Mountain, N.S." a pamphlet published by St. John's, 1963.

Doull, John, *Reverend Alexander McGillivray, D.D.*, Halifax, N.S., 1938.

Gibson, M. Allen, "Presbyterian Church, MacLellan's Mountain," The Chronicle-Herald, 1979.

Sherwood, Roland, "Cathedral Monument Erected by Congregation," The Evening News, April 8, 1961.

"MacLennan Mountain Church Marks Founding By Church Of Scotland," The Evening News, August 10, 1963.

"Church will celebrate its 163rd anniversary," The Evening News, July 24, 1980.

"Combined Service Sunday at MacLennan's Mountain," The Evening News, August 1, 1969.

Sherwood, Roland, "Flashback to a 'Cathedral' Monument," The Pictou Advocate, March 29, 1978.

"Vandals Damage Historic Church," The Evening News, September 7, 1976.

"St. Ninian's Cathedral, A Short History and Guide," a pamphlet published by St. Ninian's Cathedral, 1974.

Chisholm, Evangeline, "History of St. Ninian's Told in Centennial Year of Parish," The Evening News, November 26, 1973.

Whidden, D.G., *The Antigonish Whiddens and Brief Historical Outline of the County and Town of Antigonish*, Wolfville, 1930.

MacDonald, H.M., "Centennial Sketches, One Hundred Years Ago," The Casket, September 12, 1974.

MacDonald, H.M., "The Cathedral Story," The Casket, October 10, 1974.

"Man Behind the Myth," the Casket, October 10, 1974.

MacDonald, Bruce, "Financing St. Ninian's," The Casket, October 10, 1974.

"Notes on St. Ninian's Cathedral," The Casket, October 10, 1974.

"Founders Guide Parish," The Casket, October 10, 1974.

Johnston, A.A., "A Cathedral is Built," The Casket, October 10, 1974.

Chiasson, Paulette, "Cathedral Alterations," The Casket, October 10, 1974.

"Decorations Illustrate Love," The Casket, October 10, 1974.

"Church Bells Ring Clear," The Casket, October 10, 1974.

"Centennial Year Renovations," The Casket, October 10, 1974.

Sinclair, D.M. *Fort Massey Church, Halifax, Nova Scotia 1871-1971, A Century of Witness*, a book published by the church, 1971.

Shutlak, G., "Fort Massey is a 'unique' landmark," The Mail-Star, May 31, 1977.

Gibson, M. Allen, "Fort Massey Church, Halifax," The Chronicle-Herald, March 21, 1964.

Beaton, Josephine, *Glencoe, An Historical Sketch*, a booklet published by St. Joseph's Church, 1973.

Patterson, Rev. George, *A History of the County of Pictou, Nova Scotia*, pp. 134, 274, 429-435, facsimile edition, Mika Studio, Belleville, Ontario, 1972.

MacPhie, Rev. J.P., *Pictonians At Home and Abroad,* pp. 207, 208, 224, Pinkham Press, Boston, Massachusetts, 1914.

Cameron, James M., *Churches of New Glasgow*, The Hector Publishing Co. Ltd., New Glasgow, 1961.

"Tells Story Of The Building Of First County Churches," The Evening News, September 25, 1965.

Robertson, J. Bruce, "A History of the Presbyterian Congregations of New Glasgow, N.S.," a fact sheet published by St. Andrew's Presbyterian Church, New Glasgow.

"Century of Westminster Church in October 1948," The Eastern Chronicle, September 30, 1948.

"Westminster to celebrate 106th anniversary," The Evening News, November 29, 1980.

"Westminster to mark 104th birthday," The Evening News, October 13, 1978.

Gibson, M. Allen, "Westminster Presbyterian Church, New Glasgow," The Chronicle-Herald, April 9, 1960.

Randall, Tim, "Steeples Far And Near," a manuscript, November 1979.

Davies, Canon S.J.P., "The Reverend Simon Gibbons," a manuscript.

Prichard, Archdeacon Gregory, "Simon Gibbons," an information sheet.

Gibson, M. Allen, "St. Thomas Anglican Church, Mooseland," The Chronicle-Herald, November 22, 1980.

Gibson, M. Allen, "St. Mark's Anglican Church, Moose River," The Chronicle-Herald, April 26, 1969.

Gibson, M. Allen, "Holy Trinity Anglican Church, Jordan Falls," February 1, 1964.

Bethune, Dr. C.M., "Church of St. Peter — St. John, Baddeck, Nova Scotia," a fact sheet published by the church.

Gibson, M. Allen, "St. Peter and St. John Anglican Church, Baddeck," The Chronicle-Herald, April 1, 1978.

Hill, Fred F., "Anniversary, St. James' United Church, Great Village, Nova Scotia, 1973," a booklet published by St. James', July 1973.

Gibson, M. Allen, "United Church of Canada, Great Village," The Chronicle-Herald, October 9, 1954.

"Great Village New Presbyterian Church," The Truro Guardian, June 5, 1883.

"Colourful Past Recalled," The Chronicle-Herald, July 18, 1960.

Gibson, M. Allen, "St. James' Anglican Church, Mahone Bay," The Chronicle-Herald, June 15, 1957.

"Church Marks 100th Anniversary Sunday," The Chronicle-Herald, November 3, 1960.

Tuck, Robert C., *Gothic Dreams*, the Life and Times of a Canadian Architect, William Critchlow Harris 1854-1913, Dandurn Press Ltd., Toronto, Canada 1978.

Harris, William C., Original specifications for St. James' Church, Mahone Bay.

Joudrey, O.S., *History Summary, St. James' Parish*, published by St. James' church, c. 1960.

Joudrey, O.S., "History of St. James' Parish," The Progress Enterprise, May 16, 1962.

Toomey, Lucine, "Mahone Bay — a beautiful town," The Bridgewater Bulletin, October 26, 1977.

The Story of Five Islands, Colchester County, Nova Scotia, pp. 78-94, The Women's Institute, Five Islands, 1969.

Gibson, M. Allen, "Peniel United Church, Five Islands," The Chronicle-Herald, May 26, 1956.

Blauveldt, Robert B., *The Roman Catholic Diocese of Yarmouth, 20th Anniversary,* 1973.

Gibson, M. Allen, "The Cathedral of St. Ambrose, Yarmouth," The Chronicle-Herald, June 1, 1963.

"Saint Ambrose Cathedral, After One Hundred Years," a pamphlet published by the parish, 1957.

"La Nouvelle Eglise de St. Ambrose à Yarmouth," L'Evangéline, October 9, 1890.

"The Return of the Exiles," The Casket, April 2, 1964.

Gibson, M. Allen, "St. Peter's Roman Catholic Church, Cheticamp," The Chronicle-Herald, November 17, 1956.

Tufts, Evelyn S., "St. Peter's Roman Catholic Church," The Chronicle-Herald, August 28, 1954.

"Historical Notes on Chéticamp," a fact sheet published by St. Peter's Church.

MacSwain, J.M., *History of the Amherst Baptist Church*, First Baptist Church, 1979.

"A Magnificent New Baptist Church at Amherst," The Halifax Herald, September 24, 1894.

"Amherst Herald" The Halifax Herald, May 5, 1907.

"The Well and Favourably Known Red Stone Quarry at Amherst," The Morning Chronicle, May 11, 1901.

"Magnificent New Baptist Church," The Evening Mail, September 3, 1895.

L'Eglise Ste-Marie, a book published by St. Mary's, 1980.

Gibson, M. Allen, "St. Mary's Roman Catholic Church, Church Point," The Chronicle-Herald, February 12, 1955.

MacCrae, Genevieve, "Continent's largest wooden church to mark 75th anniversary," The Chronicle-Herald, February 25, 1980.

Saulnier, Janine, *St. Mary's Church and Parish*, 1978.

"Big Church Building Is Tourist Attraction," The Chronicle-Herald, July 15, 1960.

Credits

Drawings

1. MacFawn and Rogers Architects, pages 38, 48, 49, 92, 130, 167.
2. Architectural Resource Consultants Ltd., page 80.
3. William DeGarthe, page 97.
4. Kathleen Morrison, page 112.
5. J.C. Dumaresq, pages 143, 144
6. H.H. Mott, page 158

Photography

The majority of the photographs were taken by Elizabeth Pacey. However, photographs obtained from other sources are as follows:

1. Tim Randall, pages 46, 27, 117, 79, 120
2. Elizabeth Ross, pages 122, 124
3. Arthur Carter, page 102
4. Robert Gourley, page 90
5. St. Ninian's Cathedral, page 88
6. *The Casket*, page 94
7. Nova Scotia Government Services, 1978, pages 162, 164, 76, 146, 148, 134
8. Architectural Resource Consultants, pages 166, 21, 28, 23, 77, 21